"*Dough Nation: How Pizza (and Sm—* [text obscured by barcode] be required reading for future entrep [text obscured by barcode] deftly explains how making *giving* a co [text obscured by barcode] tangible benefits for their community, their employees, and their bottom line. I worked closely with Chris and his business partner, Max, on several events, and his commitment to collaborative philanthropy comes through with every conversation. I'm thrilled he wrote this book to spread the word about how every business can not only help but solve some of our biggest challenges."

—*Ron Wade, Director of Marketing*
Detroit Tigers (2010–2018)

"Two outside-the-box thinkers built a business around purpose and serving others. This inspiring journey demonstrates action, intentionality, and perseverance."

—*Rich Wolowski, President and CEO*
Gordon Food Service

"In *Dough Nation: How Pizza (and Small Businesses) Can Change the World*, Christopher Andrus makes a compelling case that a fulfilling life inside and outside of business is about the journey, not the finish line. And that the more people we engage with and help along our journeys, the more nourishing and impactful that journey will be. There is a lot more good karma that comes with focusing our energies around collaboration and sustainability than with focusing on competition, and Chris brings that ideal to life in every chapter of this timely book."

—*Sam Calagione, Founder and Brewer*
Dogfish Head Brewery

"*Dough Nation: How Pizza (and Small Businesses) Can Change the World* is an inspiring story of two leaders and their vision for creating a business that embodied their values and passion for helping others. They have seen tremendous success in our community and have built a growing population of loyal customers. As mayor of our amazing city, I've seen firsthand the incredible impact the Mitten Brewing Company has had on our Westside neighborhood. They stand as a powerful demonstration of what can happen when we support local businesses and they in return support our community."

—*Rosalynn Bliss, Mayor*
Grand Rapids, Michigan

"Small businesses are the backbone and economic engine of Michigan and our country. *Dough Nation: How Pizza (and Small Businesses) Can Change the World* is a great example of how Chris Andrus (and his partner, Max Trierweiler) built a successful small business through entrepreneurship, outside-the-box thinking, and a focus on giving back to his community. By following this blueprint, the Mitten Brewing Company has become a staple in Michigan's growing brewing industry. Chris's vision and commitment to philanthropy illustrate the power a small business can have in the surrounding community and the world."

—*Senator Gary C. Peters*

"In this interesting and spirited book, Chris writes about the incredible impact that small businesses can make in their communities through partnerships with nonprofits. Chris rightly asserts that good works are good for business. Untethered by the practices and priorities of large corporations, privately owned businesses can create meaningful and long-term partnerships that advance their partners' causes, while fostering goodwill with their intensely loyal customers. Customers and employees rally around businesses that stand for something, and nonprofits are the grateful beneficiaries of this growing philosophy."

—*Julie Pendell, Vice President*
Make-A-Wish Michigan

DOUGH
NATION

FOREWORD BY GRAND RAPIDS MAYOR ROSALYNN BLISS

DOUGH
NATION

HOW PIZZA (AND SMALL BUSINESSES) CAN CHANGE THE WORLD

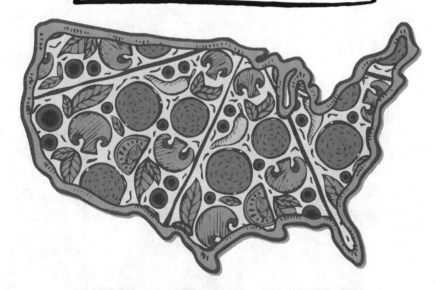

CHRISTOPHER ANDRUS

CO-OWNER OF THE MITTEN BREWING COMPANY
FOUNDER OF MITTEN FOUNDATION, INC.

PRINCIPIA
MEDIA

Dough Nation
©2020 Christopher Andrus

Principia Media, LLC
678 Front Avenue NW
Suite 256
Grand Rapids MI 49504
(www.principiamedia.com)

ISBN 978-1-61485-008-3

24 23 22 21 20 19   7 6 5 4 3 2 1

Printed in the United States of America

Edited by Patti Waldygo, Desert Sage Editorial Services
Cover design by Shannon Andrus
Interior layout by Frank Gutbrod
Author photo by Terry Johnston

CONTENTS

························

FOREWORD

....

SMALL BUSINESS IS THE heart and soul of a local economy and often becomes a significant part of the fabric of a neighborhood. *Dough Nation: How Pizza (and Small Businesses) Can Change the World* is the story of just that: a small, locally owned business created with a deep commitment and intention to focus on more than just its bottom line. From the early inception of their business, owners Christopher Andrus and Max Trierweiler had a vision for creating a company that had a heart for community, a dedication to making their neighborhood a better place, and a desire to establish a culture of giving back. It is a culture built on a love for people and a fundamental belief that a business needs to invest in people and causes they believe in.

Dough Nation is an inspiring story of two leaders and their vision for creating a business that embodied their values and passion for helping others. They have seen tremendous success in our community and have built a growing population of loyal customers. As mayor of our amazing city, I've seen firsthand the incredible impact the Mitten Brewing Company has had on our Westside neighborhood. The Mitten played a key role in its revitalization when the company invested in an old firehouse and brought it back

1

to life as a destination for great beer and great food, making it a place where everyone feels welcome. Beyond that, the Mitten stands as a powerful demonstration of what can happen when we support local businesses and they in return support our community.

We are extremely fortunate to have author Christopher R. Andrus, co-owner of the Mitten Brewing Company and founder of the 501(c)(3) Mitten Foundation, Inc., in Grand Rapids. Chris is an authentic servant leader who leads by example and is humble, kind, and passionate about helping others. Andrus made a conscious and deliberate decision to use his business as a force for good and has shown that a business truly can focus on the triple bottom line—people, planet, and profit. Besides growing his brewery from a small startup to a $4-plus million company with three locations and more than a hundred employees, Chris and his business partner, Max Trierweiler, have presided over more than $250,000 in charitable gifts since 2012. These pages are filled with heart-warming stories of lives that have been impacted by their philanthropy. From the children who participate in the Inner-City Youth Baseball and Softball program to the little girl who had her wish come true with Make-A-Wish Michigan, we are given real-life examples of the power of a business working for good.

Our community is a better place because of people like Christopher Andrus and the Mitten Brewing Company. As you enjoy this powerful read, may you also think of ways you can have a greater impact on your own community. Thank you, Chris, for sharing your story and for making a compelling case about how America's small businesses can change the world.

Cheers,
Rosalynn Bliss
Mayor, City of Grand Rapids

AUTHOR'S NOTE

....

> "I CONSIDER MYSELF THE LUCKIEST MAN
> ON THE FACE OF THE EARTH."
> — LOU GEHRIG

LET ME BEGIN by saying I was born on third base.

I know I didn't hit a triple.

I don't mean to say I didn't work hard because I did. Growing the Mitten Brewing Company with my business partner and friend, Max Trierweiler, has been the achievement of my life. Together, we built our company from the ground up. We scraped together small investments, went long periods without paying ourselves, and barely cleared payroll more times than we can count. We fought and overcame all the tribulations undercapitalized startups face every day.

But we know we're lucky.

We come from well-off families. We are surrounded by people who, with a little persuasion, gave us their hard-earned money to fund our dream. We opened our brewery during craft beer's historic renaissance. Our customers were patient with us as we dialed in our offerings, and we have been all but overwhelmed with business since the day we opened our doors.

3

But most of all, we started our company in one of the most affluent countries in the world. While nearly half the planet lives on less than $6 a day (Howton, 2018), here people like us have the opportunity to make a comfortable living doing something we love. We can't take credit for that. It is an incredible luxury to be who we are, where we are, when we are. It is also a great responsibility.

Along with this capacity for extraordinary wealth comes devastating inequality. Everywhere we look, we see people marginalized by institutional poverty and discrimination. There are far too many for whom hunger is a daily challenge and countless children who do not have their most basic needs met. These people don't exist in the abstract; in the cracks of every city in the world, they are very much alive. And they need help.

Even in the earliest versions of our business plan, Max and I were committed to charitable giving. We weren't sure exactly what shape it would take, but the choice was important to us. We wanted to build our business in a neighborhood and create a symbiotic relationship with the people who surrounded us. We hoped our existence would make their lives better. Many twists, countless turns, and a huge learning curve later, we're now on our way to making a bigger difference than we ever thought possible. Our seven years of giving—including the four before we formed our nonprofit Mitten Foundation in 2017—taught us many things, but none more important (and surprising) than the fact that giving has actually been the driving force behind our extraordinary success.

I became motivated to write a book about philanthropy. I felt the voice of the small business owner was missing in the canon. Yet although I was eager to share the realizations we had unlocked, I wasn't sure whether I was qualified. After all, I'm not a professional philanthropist, nor do I have decades of business experience.

I didn't want my message to come across as hubris. During the course of writing this book, this uncertainty of purpose led me to dead end after dead end. So I studied other works for inspiration, mostly memoirs and leadership books. I read a few I figured might be corollaries but quickly came to a painful conclusion:

This is useless.

Though I enjoy reading books about luminaries like Steve Jobs and Lee Iacocca, the gulf between them and me is just too great. These fascinating stories chronicle the lives of inspiring figures, sure, but aren't they once-in-a-generation talents? Isn't a lot about what made them successful ineffable? How can I apply their experience to my daily work as the co-owner of a regional brewery, right here and, more important, *right now*? As I've seen even in my short career, things change more quickly than conventional wisdom is able to recognize or adjust to. Status quos are ephemeral and are often upended within years, not lifetimes. There are serious limits to what we can learn from the career retrospectives of humanity's unusually successful outliers.

In this, I found my purpose: to demonstrate the value of sharing gains *as we experience them*, not at the end of our careers and lives. How else can we truly expect others to benefit from them? I hoped to show how we defined our small company by giving, and I wanted to do it from my unique vantage point as someone the reader could actually meet and (hopefully) relate to. Someone who has had success but is very much still in the thick of his entrepreneurial journey. Someone who aspires to give with purpose. Someone who understands both the limits and the opportunities of the time in which we live. I hope that for you, I am this person.

To accomplish this, I had to find my stories. It was a challenge; although I lived them, I learned I hadn't spent enough time considering them. I didn't realize just how much had happened in the last seven years. Though arduous, the writing process was enlightening, and I ended up with a very different book than the one I set out to create. Yet it was a better one. Writing a book is a lot like starting a business. Clarity of purpose—essential to both—often takes time to develop. And I'm glad I took that time. I met with nonprofit leaders in my community. I surveyed our customers. I spoke to my staff. I studied volumes about the history of philanthropy in the United States. I wrote and rewrote. Ultimately, I gained a greater understanding of why companies like ours have such an important role to play in the future of philanthropy. Though I consider the Mitten Brewing Company to be special, it's because in many respects, *we're not*. There are 30 million companies just like us. This isn't pejorative; our strength is in our numbers and our shared ideals.

I am convinced that while America's nonprofits are still best suited to do the great work of our lifetime, the country's small businesses—not its wealthy corporations—will become the engine that drives them. Only in the fabric of these agile and conscientious companies reside the heart, the understanding, and the scale that are necessary to ensure a prosperous future for our nation's nonprofits.

As I'll show in this book, companies like ours are rooted in their communities in a way that large corporations never could be. They're made up of entrepreneurs, friends, and neighbors of all walks of life. Hardly anyone is rich. *But it's our time.* As customers continue to become more educated, ethical, and local-centric about the purchases they make, the opportunity for companies like ours has never been greater, and neither has our ability to pay it forward. I fully believe entrepreneurship will save the world. The path may be crooked and the pace dizzying, but the time is now. The people are us.

For nearly a decade before I ever considered starting my own business, I was a professional musician. Music was how I connected to the world, and writing songs was how I expressed its beauty and pain. I didn't believe there was any other way to feel as deeply about something. But when I came to the point where I was too tired and destitute to continue, I knew I had to find another way to achieve meaning in my professional life. I never imagined it would be this. Yet through this company, I've experienced more creation, passion, and purpose than I ever thought possible, and I was able to feel every bit as deeply about it. I learned that in the end, it doesn't matter what you do as long as you do it in a way that brings meaning and joy to those who are involved.

And that's what giving has done for me. It's brought depth and purpose to my professional life, which, I've learned through my thirty-nine years on this planet, I need to survive. And I know I'm not alone. Our increasingly interconnected world has paradoxically created a life of isolation and discontentment for many—even the successful. I don't mean to sound ungrateful, but the contentment that typically comes from owning a profitable business, paying bills on time, and driving a car that doesn't break down once a week isn't enough for me. Though I'm thankful for those things because they all still feel a bit foreign, I need more. The overriding impulse to do something great is what attracted me to music in the first place; it was a rebuke to the callous desire to make money for money's sake. I may have been young and idealistic, but I truly wanted to do nothing more than create beautiful and inspiring things and make a difference in people's lives. I saw only one way to do it back then. But now I'm living proof we can imbue purpose into anything we choose, even beer and pizza.

What follows is the story of a small company that learned not only how to give well beyond its means, but also how to unlock the staggering potential that lies within each of America's smallest companies. It's full of successes, failures, and well-intentioned missteps, but it's ultimately a tale of individuals bound by the common desire to make their lives and communities better and what it takes to get there. It is a journey that, although very much still in progress, has taught me about the extraordinary faith that customers place in businesses like ours and how this faith grants us, when joined with our peers, the ability to ultimately move the needle on the systemic problems that plague us. Best of all, we can do so while making our businesses stronger and more competitive in the process.

In short, I don't want to uproot Corporate America. I want to *root* small business—in perhaps the most worthy of missions.

—Chris Andrus, October 4, 2019

INTRODUCTION

·······················

ONE SUMMER IN *the village, the people gathered for a picnic. As they shared food and conversation, someone noticed a baby in the river, struggling and crying. The baby was going to drown!*

Someone rushed to save the baby. Then they noticed another screaming baby in the river, and they pulled that baby out. Soon, more babies were seen drowning in the river, and the townspeople were pulling them out as fast as they could. It took great effort, and they began to organize their activities in order to save the babies as they came down the river. As everyone else was busy in the rescue efforts to save the babies, two of the townspeople started to run away along the shore of the river.

"Where are you going?" shouted one of the rescuers. "We need your help to save these babies!"

"We are going upstream to stop whoever is throwing them in!"

"The Parable of the River" (FAS Arizona, 2018), popularized by community organizer Saul Alinsky but likely adapted from a story by Irving Zola, is powerful. It illustrates how the battle to combat social ills is fought on multiple fronts. It demonstrates the heart that moves us to give, the urgency that forces us to act, and the perspective we must acquire in order to solve difficult problems. It also shows us that philanthropy, like anything else, evolves over time.

Charity is in a predicament, nationally. Though overall giving totals continue to increase alongside the nation's gross domestic product (Charity Navigator, 2018), the *number* of people who give is falling dramatically (Osili and Zarins, 2018) because the main avenues that have traditionally encouraged it—whether they be religion, marriage, single-occupation careers, or home ownership— among the non-rich are disappearing, especially in younger generations. High-dollar charitable giving is now done more by the solitary rich, and, with a few notable exceptions, large corporations and wealthy individuals donate primarily to organizations *outside* of the social services.

A 2012 article published by the *Atlantic* noted that "of the 50 largest individual gifts to public charities in 2012, 34 went to educational institutions, the vast majority of them colleges and universities, like Harvard, Columbia, and Berkeley, that cater to the nation's and the world's elite. Museums and arts organizations such as the Metropolitan Museum of Art received nine of these major gifts, with the remaining donations spread among medical facilities and fashionable charities like the Central Park Conservancy" (Stern, 2013).

Not a single one of these top thirty-four gifts went to improve the lives of the poor. Not even the world's largest social service organizations—United Way, the Salvation Army, and Feeding America—benefited. As the wealthiest 1 percent of Americans continue to get richer, the wealth gap in philanthropy will likely only get bigger, a trend demonstrated by the rise of Fidelity Charitable, the donor-advised fund that surpassed United Way to become the largest U.S. charity in 2016 (Swanson, 2016). This is a "charity" that gives to no one cause in particular; rather, its donors establish giving accounts and deposit funds they can write off immediately but don't have to direct toward a nonprofit until a later date, sometimes years into the future. This type of giving is disproportionately favored by the rich—the median account at Fidelity Charitable holds $15,000 at any given time—and funds like these have grown significantly in recent years while social services charities have seen their totals shrink (Te, 2017). Critics of funds such as Fidelity Charitable say their primary objective is tax sheltering for donors. Intention and specificity take on secondary roles.

But before we take too bleak of a view on the outlook for philanthropy, it's important to understand that the wealthy have *never* been the driving force for need-based giving in America. While they may donate heavily to the causes they prefer, they still don't give nearly as much, relative to their income, as the bottom 20 percent of wage earners in the United States. Poor Americans donate nearly *three times* as much of their resources as rich Americans do, and it is usually to organizations that seek to improve the lives of people living in extreme poverty.

The counterintuitive relationship between wealth and giving has long puzzled sociologists. In an effort to better understand it, Paul Piff, research psychologist at the University of California, Berkeley, conducted extensive experiments on how altruism relates to income class (Miller, 2012). He concluded that individuals with lower incomes generally possess more empathy, compassion, and sensitivity than those who earn higher wages and, because they are often surrounded by people in need, are more likely to act on these feelings. Piff's studies strongly suggest our actions are affected by the people nearest to us, and there is hard science to support it: other studies have shown our brain chemistry actually changes when we interact with others. As a result of strong and repeated social engagement with a person or a group, the brain releases the hormone *oxytocin,* which reduces stress and causes an uptick in emotions such as affection and generosity. In other words, familiarity plays a key role in our ability to relate to one another positively.

Conversely, according to Piff, the relentless drive to amass personal wealth—a key character trait among the wealthy—may create a tendency to behave unethically. In an interview with *New York Magazine*, he stated that his studies suggest "the rich are way more likely to prioritize their own self-interests above the interests of other people." Piff's research also shows a strong correlation between our generosity and our awareness of the needs of our surroundings. It suggests goodwill toward others isn't something that can be mandated or even necessarily encouraged; it must evolve organically over time as the result of repeated social engagements. This mirrors the thinking of philosopher Adam Smith who, in his book *The Theory of Moral Sentiments*, argues that our very sense of morality is a product of our social nature. Though we may be endowed with some natural sympathies, our closeness to one another is what brings them out. This closeness has a major effect on intentional giving, and, fortunately for its future, America's small businesses have a lot in common with the nation's generous poor.

With median incomes for self-employed Americans at incorporated businesses at $50,347 and unincorporated ones at less than half of that, it's clear that when we talk about small business owners, we're not talking about the wealthiest 1 percent, generally (SBA, 2012). So what exactly does it mean to be a small business in America? The Small Business Administration (SBA) defines a small business as any company with fewer than 500 employees. I know what you're thinking: 499 employees doesn't seem very small—and it isn't. But nearly three-quarters of America's small businesses actually have fewer than 100 employees, and most don't employ anyone apart from the owners.

Ranging from 80 to 100 employees (depending on the season), the Mitten Brewing Company is fairly representative of the category. Small companies like ours employ nearly half the workforce in the United States and represent 99.9 percent of all businesses by organizational type. And like the poor in our communities, they give. Forty-two percent of the 30 million small business owners in the United States will each give up to $1,000 to charity next year (Sophy, 2016). Representing annual totals as high as $13 billion, it's clear that although their incomes are small, their potential impact on the world is anything but.

Small businesses are the intersection where our humanity meets the marketplace. For the same reasons the poor give proportionately more than the wealthy, the people who own small businesses are uniquely suited to give. Connectedness to their surroundings, the intimate relationships that companies with fewer employees experience, and the modest earnings involved are all contributing factors. As Piff's studies show, the lives of those who give simply intersect more with those of the people they help.

Yet this is more than just happenstance. Giving is an expression of values, and entrepreneurs work to build their entire lives around their values. Very few start their own companies because they expect it to be easy. I can speak from experience that the adage "an entrepreneur is someone who works 80 hours per week to avoid working 40 for someone else" is all too true. Entrepreneurs like us are created the moment we realize we can no longer spend our time making someone *else* richer and freer. Max and I did hard physical labor every day for nearly nine months without a paycheck because of the magnetic pull of autonomy. We sought a deeper professional purpose, and entrepreneurship and giving are where we found it.

Ultimately, *giving is our business.* It's the crux of the socioeconomic contract that we as small business owners tacitly enter into with our customers daily: They sustain us at higher price points and lower efficiencies than our larger and more convenient competitors, so we sustain them by giving *more.* More depth, more meaning, more satisfaction, and more community value. Unlike many bigger companies, we cannot merely take.

Though I'm a great believer in capitalism, it cannot thrive without social conscience if America is to endure as the land of opportunity for all. The doctrine of unfettered self-interest propounded by Ayn Rand (et al.) is nonsensical to most small businesses. We lack the economies of scale to win price wars, nor can we tolerate disregard for the welfare of our customers, employees, and neighbors and expect to survive. This is why we are such an intriguing capitalist anomaly: our success depends not on competitive economic advantage but rather on ethics and relationships. A 2017 study reported, "87% of Americans would purchase a company's product because they stood up for or advocated for an issue they care about" (Cone Communications, 2017). Statistics like these show that although objective value is still important, the subjective looms larger every day.

Like entrepreneurship, giving has been a journey for me. Though the lessons we've learned have been painful at times, they ultimately convinced me that small businesses like ours are the great hope for giving in America. The sheer number of these companies, combined with their community focus, ethical practices, and strong employee relationships, has the potential to reverse charitable giving's downward trend. But doing so depends on understanding the ways in which the world is changing.

Giving used to be a function of what we earned. As previous generations rose through the professional ranks at a single company, they earned more and gave more, but the desire for that sort of trajectory is all but a relic of the past. An entire generation is leaving the American workforce as a new one comes of age, and this new one searches for meaning and fulfillment in *all things*, but perhaps none more so than the ways in which they spend their time and money.

Charities have been to some extent dispossessed by this new generation. Millennials don't give the way their parents did. *But they do give.* They do so even though they are burdened with high unemployment, low wages, and crushing student loan debt. They just give differently. They choose products with benefits. They value the environment. They give their time. They seek sustainability. They long to benefit the world in new and innovative ways, and the institutions that can most benefit haven't caught up yet. These consumers are going to change the world through the *marketplace*, and small businesses—which can most meet them where they are and in the habits they have—will be their instrument.

"The Parable of the River" perfectly illustrates the evolution of an organization's philanthropy. Before we have the resources and knowledge to effectively attack the systemic conditions that create the problems we confront, there is plenty to be gained by helping those who need it now. The longer a conscientious organization survives and improves, the better equipped it will be to ultimately *solve problems*. Much like starting a business, giving begins with heart and grows thanks to an unquenchable thirst to innovate and improve. The harder we work, the more we understand that *we can do it all.* We can save the babies floating down the river, nurture them as they grow, and work beside them to prevent babies from ever being thrown in again. We also can make our own lives better in the process. What an incredible opportunity!

This is a historic time. Since our journey through the twenty-first century began, we have witnessed the near-complete erosion of faith in many of America's most venerable institutions. Trust in government has all but disappeared, and "too big to fail" blue chip corporations, some of them still relics of the industry consolidations of the previous century, continue to collapse in front of our very eyes. This destruction is natural. The phoenix rises, and the small business has emerged as America's brightest and arguably greatest institution. Joined with our nation's youngest consumers, it also represents the future of giving. Although philanthropy has long been considered the purview of the rich and retired robber barons, the millions of small businesses in the United States in fact possess more of the resources, desire, and hard-wired characteristics needed to revolutionize giving in America. And when joined in the missions of our nation's great nonprofits, they will.

ACKNOWLEDGMENTS

....

Writing a book—especially one's first—is a daunting task, and this wouldn't have been possible without the patience and support of my loved ones. I'd like to thank:

My wife, Shannon, and sons, August and Jude, for always inspiring me to do great things.

My business partner and friend, Max, without whom this story would never have been told. Thanks for taking a risk and going on this journey with me.

My parents, Larry and Celia, for raising me to care about the right things.

Dana, our tireless board president. Your dedication to taking care of our neighbors continues to impress.

Kay VanAntwerpen, Jim Davis, Amber Eby, and Troy Reimink—their contributions to this book were immeasurable. They didn't let me get away with anything and kept sending me back in until it was right. They made this a better book, and for that I am eternally grateful. And tired. But mostly grateful.

Joe Boomgaard. From editing our high school paper to helping me put together this book, you have always demonstrated peerless dedication to journalistic integrity. Thank you for your guidance.

Our nonprofit partners. Keep doing the work, and keep challenging us to find new ways to be a part of it.

To the Mitten staff—past, present, and future. You are this company. Cheers!

GETTING STARTED

> "THERE ARE THREE TYPES OF BASEBALL PLAYERS:
> THOSE WHO MAKE IT HAPPEN, THOSE WHO WATCH IT
> HAPPEN AND THOSE WHO WONDER WHAT HAPPENS."
> — TOMMY LASORDA

"ARE YOU READY FOR this?" I asked my best friend and aspiring business partner, Max Trierweiler. We were huddled in the corner of a back room in a downstairs office building. Outside, the autumn sun had set, and the office was dark, save for the fluorescent overheads. Behind us, our friend Matt was unboxing pizzas, and our wives were cutting them into small squares and putting them on paper plates.

"As ready as I'm gonna be," Max said. We fist-bumped nervously, took a deep breath, and walked out to meet our guests.

On September 18, 2011, Max and I held the first of two investor presentations in the basement of his father's office. Several weeks earlier, we had mailed out invitations to anyone we thought might be a candidate for investment and asked that person to bring someone else who fit the same profile. We set up folding tables and a projector as we waited for our twenty or so guests to arrive. As they found their seats, we walked them through our business plan, stopping periodically to discuss the beer and pizza pairings that would eventually be featured at a new startup we were calling the Mitten Brewing Company.

We intended the presentation to be polished and professional, but it was meandering at best. And this was revealed during the question-and-answer portion. A guest criticized us for not having a clear-enough vision for the company, for trying to be "all things to all people." And that stuck with us. We didn't raise much money, and we went back to the drawing board to prepare for the next presentation.

An important event did occur that night, however—one that would change the company forever. But first, who were these two 31-year-old men asking strangers for money?

For nearly a decade prior to that evening, I had been a professional singer and songwriter. I toured the country, released six albums, and even attracted the attention of major recording labels. But after my long final push that included playing more than 150 shows per year, recording and promoting endlessly, and sleeping on couches, pool tables, and floors throughout the country, the elusive recording contract failed to materialize. It was time to do something else.

Max and I had been friends since first grade, when we met and attended a small Catholic school together. He had been doing marketing for my father's company for seven years and was ready to make a career change. Although neither of us had any professional brewing or hospitality experience, we knew we wanted to do something together. On impulse, we purchased a home-brewing kit from Siciliano's Market, our local homebrew supply shop.

Any home brewer will admit the hobby starts innocently enough but eventually becomes an all-consuming black hole of fermentation vessels, instruments, meters, hoses, and coils. Not to mention the complete forfeiture of a home's kitchen and closets. The smart ones move it out to the garage, which is what we did. And we went all in. We bought all the textbooks we could find and brewed endlessly, often the same style of beer over and over again, always seeking professional quality. We framed out walls, ran plumbing, and installed refrigeration. Some people home-brew to have fun and relax; *that was not us*. We were fanatical about it.

When we decided to make our dream a reality, we weren't exactly sure how to start. The movies led us to believe the first step was to apply for a bank loan, but some quick research revealed that most restaurants and bars, due to the high anecdotal failure rate and inherent risks involved, are almost exclusively financed with private capital. Traditional debt financing wasn't really a viable option anyway because in 2011, banks were not eager to lend to anybody, much less former musicians. This was only two years after the housing collapse and the 2009 recession. But we tried anyway and failed, so we turned our focus to private investors.

We knew we had to put together a strong business plan—one that excited investors and clearly defined a path to success—but we lacked a unique vision, which we unexpectedly found on my thirty-first birthday. On April 16, 2011, Max and I set out to find a place to watch our beloved Detroit Tigers and drink the craft beers we liked. After walking in and out of what seemed like countless establishments that evening, we concluded that this place, as we imagined it, didn't really exist. Elitist craft beer bars typically eschewed sporting events, and sports bars at that time had little to no relationship with great beer. We just wished for something in between, and we realized that was what we wanted to create. With our vision of a brewery where both sports enthusiasts and customers new to craft beer would feel welcome, we were ready to start writing our business plan.

We knew we wouldn't have as much money as, well, anyone, so we put our emphasis on standing out from the pack. One way we hoped to do that was by charitable giving. It was a value Max and I both shared, and we thought it would be an interesting way to set ourselves apart. Though I'd like to say we had a clearer idea than that, we really didn't. We had no idea how much of a role giving would play in the life of our company. I suppose it's a testament to always leading with your heart. You never know where you might end up, but at least you know it was for the right reasons.

Writing a business plan is an exhilarating but daunting process. Though a blank page can be paralyzing to some, we saw it as an opportunity to make the Mitten exactly what we wanted it to be. We worked hard to make sure our lives and interests were incorporated into our plan, and most of our giving mission was informed by my personal experience. Although my music career had me spending most of my nights in bars, I spent my days working with children who had developmental disabilities.

My connection to this work was especially deep because I had a lifetime of familiarity. I have two younger brothers, the youngest of whom was diagnosed with autism spectrum disorder in 1990. This was a life-changing event that threw our family headlong into the special needs community and gave everyone, but mostly my parents, the challenge of our lives. My parents became heavily involved in the nonprofit world, focusing on providing services for families afflicted with autism. My brother Josh is a truly special and talented person, and we can't imagine our lives without him, despite the challenges. My love for him and anguish over his daily struggles galvanized my desire to make life better for those in need.

My wife, Shannon, also has spent most of her career as an art instructor for adults and students with severe disabilities. Every day she gives deeply of her time, supplies, and considerable expertise. But she doesn't just teach; she changes lives. She has turned students who have never created a piece of art into working artists. She's helped my brother Josh win multiple art competitions. She's even taught quadriplegics to paint with their teeth. She's a beautiful, talented person, and I love her dearly.

But back to that night in September 2011.

We spent some time describing our rather ill-defined giving program to the group, and judging from the murmurs of approval, this seemed like one of the aspects of our presentation that resonated well. At the end of the evening, we handed out investment forms to all attendees and waited sheepishly to see if anyone would cut us a check. My body flushed with panic as we watched most of the guests shuffle out the door without doing so. A few did, but they were the people we were already counting on. We noticed one guest lingering in the back corner, speaking quietly on his phone. After the room had emptied, he walked up to us with a check written for our highest investment level. "Sorry it took so long," he said. "I had to call my financial adviser to see how much I could invest. I just wish it was more."

He told us he was so moved by our commitment to charity that he simply had to be a part of what we were building. We were speechless. We had never met the man—he was a guest of a guest—but we had connected on a level that went beyond a mere investment strategy. He had never heard of a business making this sort of commitment before it opened, and that's what made the difference for him.

We went home that evening with our heads spinning about what had worked and what hadn't. With less than two weeks until the next presentation, we knew we had a lot of feedback to consider, but there was one thing we knew for sure: we needed to further develop our ideas for giving. The first presentation showed us we were not alone in recognizing the value of building philanthropy into the company. But overall, there had been far more misses than hits. While the mistakes were painful to relive, they forced us to clarify our vision, and we spent the next few weeks carefully eliminating sections of our bloated two-hour presentation. The only area we ended up expanding on was giving.

We added a new incentive for our investors: If they invested during this first round of fundraising, they could handpick one of the charities we would support in our first year. They just had to choose a group they had a connection to, and we would make a company donation in their name. They were even invited to help us present the giant novelty check. This strategy made all the difference in the world.

We knew we had tapped into something special when we asked for questions at the end of the second presentation and not a single hand went up. Max and I grinned when we saw that most guests already had their checkbooks out. Though we continued raising money until the day we opened (and even a little afterward), we had enough to get started. I learned that at the end of the day, *people invest in people*. It's a gut feeling, and what it ultimately comes down to is whether someone believes in us, identifies with what we're doing, and feels confident intertwining his or her future with ours. I'm certain our commitment to charity helped foster that faith in our investors. As soon as we got our heads around that and developed a little swagger, the investments started rolling in, and by the time we opened, we were actually turning people away.

Why was giving so important to our investors? Why was it so crucial to earning their trust and money? And why were we moved to make it such an important part of our company? Because deep within all of us is the understanding that giving is what connects us to one another and advances the course of humanity.

In one form or another, philanthropy has always existed in our world. After his death in the fourth century BCE, the Greek philosopher Plato left his farm to a relative and instructed him to use the proceeds to benefit the students and the faculty of the Academy in Athens. In fact, the word *philanthropy* comes from the Greek, meaning "love of mankind."

Philosophers and religious scholars alike recognize the necessity of giving. Buddhism, Hinduism, and the three Abrahamic religions consider it a duty of all adherents (Levy, 2012, and Sugirtharajah, 2001). Both St. Thomas Aquinas and German philosopher Immanuel Kant agreed that reason is the source of morality, and reason demands we practice charity (Winchester, 2015). Kant considered it a *categorical imperative* (Kant, 1785).

Philanthropy may be part of the very fabric of the people and the land that would become America. In the early seventeenth century, Patuxet native North American Tisquantum ("Squanto") played a pivotal role in the survival of the ill-prepared colonists at Plymouth, Massachusetts (Brooks, 2012). Though he had been abducted and sold into slavery by an Englishman less than a decade earlier, he still honored the long-held Native American tradition of giving by teaching the Pilgrims to fish and grow corn. His extraordinary and selfless acts made it possible for the fledgling settlement to thrive.

Alexis de Tocqueville, the French scholar and political scientist, wrote that "voluntary associations," which he defined as "private initiatives for public good, focusing on quality of life," were an inborn and unique feature in American culture and an irreplaceable attribute in the success of its democracy (De Tocqueville, 1835). In his seminal 1835 work *Democracy in America*, de Tocqueville observed that "in the United States associations are established to promote public order, commerce, industry, morality, and religion; for there is no end which the human will, seconded by the collective exertions of individuals, despairs of attaining."

Yet most relevant to this story, making a commitment to giving in the fall of 2011 provided us with the investment we needed to move our brewery out of my garage on Elmer Street and out into the great wide world. Neither Max nor I was sure if we were truly ready, but we were as ready as we were going to be.

CHAPTER 2

OPENING DAY

·····················

> "BASEBALL IS A ROOKIE. HIS EXPERIENCE NO BIGGER
> THAN THE LUMP IN HIS THROAT AS HE BEGINS
> FULFILLMENT OF HIS DREAM."
> — ERNIE HARWELL

"WE SHOULD STAY HERE, tonight!" I said, as I slid down the brass fire pole. Our realtor Chad chuckled at the quote from *Ghostbusters*. It was January 2012, and Max and I were touring Engine House No. 9, a decommissioned Victorian brick firehouse on the west edge of Grand Rapids. We had admired the old building for years but until that day had never actually been inside it. The closest I'd been was when Shannon and I used to park behind it while my band played Juke's Bar across the street. But we loved it and were certain we had found our home. The engine house had been extensively remodeled (*remuddled*, one might say) since it went into private use in 1966, but its potential was obvious. To us, at least.

Some of our investors would express misgivings about our choice of location in the coming weeks, and it wasn't hard to see why. "Craft brewery" wasn't the first thing that came to mind when surveying our block. The homeless mingled with prostitutes at the corner bus stop, trash blew around like tumbleweeds, and busy Leonard Street was more like an airport runway than a pedestrian thoroughfare. But Max and I had toured breweries across the country, and we knew reclaiming old buildings and neighborhoods was a common theme in the world of craft. We were hopeful our unique setting and mission would help people find us, wherever we were.

But we knew it wasn't going to be easy. As we looked around the dusty old firehouse, we were nervous about the amount of work ahead of us. The building had to be gutted, right down to its bones, and all of the electrical and HVAC redone. It was definitely going to take more time than we thought. And money. Once we got into the project, the capital we had raised got spent in a hurry. We could have raised more, but we didn't want to be on the hook for any more than we already were. We knew that if we were going to get across the finish line, we would have to find a way to accomplish a lot with a little.

· · · · · · · · · · · · · · · · · · · ·

From the very beginning, we had set our sights on Grand Rapids' West Side. "The West Side" is its own borough, of sorts. Defined locally as any area of town west of the Grand River—the large river that bisects the city and attracted city founder Louis Campau to settle there in 1826—the West Side is a blue-collar community, dense with immigrant families and descendants of the people who worked in the once-bustling furniture factories that made the city famous. In 2011, the area was heavily populated and full of blight. It was ripe for investment, in our view. The West

Side hadn't been home to a working brewery since Prohibition, and though most of its properties needed work, they were unique and historic. Plus, the opportunities for giving were plentiful. Here in this neighborhood was another chance to stand out.

Property values were low, compared to the rest of the city, and we were able to buy the engine house for an affordable price. We were in love with it, even though it quickly became love-hate. The next eight months were a nightmare at times. Getting the 120-year-old building up to code was quite a challenge, especially since we did most of the work ourselves. The days were long—often twelve to sixteen hours—and made even longer when Shannon gave birth to our first son, a colicky little ball of fire named August. Our customers were quite familiar with the curly-haired toddler running around the taproom in the early years. We love him to death, but the timing probably couldn't have been worse. Rest was a rare commodity in the Andrus household. Shannon often tells the story of the time she came into August's room in the middle of the night to find me in the rocking chair, half-asleep and rocking an imaginary child in my arms. August was snoozing in his crib, unaware. I don't even remember it.

Max and I built the tables, sandblasted the walls, and pieced together the bar from tongue-and-groove boards reclaimed from the demolition process. The days were long and dirty, and the slow tempo of progress was discouraging. Max and I grew frustrated—with the process and each other—and words we didn't mean were exchanged more than a few times. Costs continued to mount, and it seemed like every time we turned around, we were meeting with another investor and further diluting our share of ownership. We came up with a "lite" version of our investment presentation that we delivered many times onsite during the construction phase, often with soot-stained faces and clothes. We were exhausted, but we kept grinding.

People often ask me what, if anything, we would have done differently getting started, and I used to say we would have raised more money and hired contractors so we wouldn't have had to push ourselves so hard, but I don't feel that way anymore. Now that we're on the other side of it, there's something to be said about the pride we feel when we look across our taproom and realize we built all those things, instead of ordering them out of a catalog. It becomes part of our story, and because of this, we know every inch of the building and the neighborhood. We got to know our neighbors intimately because we talked to them every day as we sawed wood on the sidewalk. We shared beers with them as they poked their heads inside to see what we were up to. We're grateful to be a part of our neighborhood for many reasons, but none more so than the people we've been fortunate to meet—sometimes in unexpected ways.

NUMBER 49

Winter Beer Fest is a uniquely Michigan event. Organized annually by the Michigan Brewers Guild, this beer festival is renowned because it's entirely outdoors. In Michigan. In February. Of course, that doesn't stop thousands of hearty craft beer enthusiasts from suiting up in insulated coveralls, Viking hats, and pretzel necklaces to drink rare Michigan beers. Though we weren't open yet, Max and I excitedly bought tickets to the 2012 WBF weeks in advance and were eager to spend the day rubbing elbows with Michigan's brewing elite.

But on the day of the festival, I didn't want to go. I didn't want to do anything, in fact. Earlier that morning, we had put our family dog to sleep. I was awakened by a call from my father who told me that Sparky, our elderly white Lhasa Apso named for famed Detroit Tigers manager Sparky Anderson, was having grand mal seizures, one after the other.

I got dressed and drove to their house. My parents were adamant that it was time to put him down, but my brother Brad and I were conflicted. Sparky was twenty, old even by old dog standards, but was still eating and drinking. We were hoping for a sign—something to make the decision easy—and after we comforted him through a final long and heartbreaking seizure, we all knew it was time. We took him to the vet together and tearfully held him as the vet administered the euthanasia drug. His arthritic body relaxed as the medicine coursed through him, and we knew we made the right choice. He had been in pain for a long time. I went home and, after several minutes of staring at the Beer Fest ticket on the kitchen counter, decided to go. What else was I going to do? I was sad about Sparky, but after all, he had a pretty good run. I put on my warm clothes and went to meet Max.

We walked around the festival with a bit of a secret: nobody knew we would soon be brewery owners. We had signed the lease on the engine house only weeks prior and had just begun the demolition process. We drank, introduced ourselves to brewers, and engaged in dozens of the tipsy conversations with strangers you have only at beer festivals. Huddled around one of the parking lot bonfires, we met a man named Paul. When we told him we were starting the first brewery on the West Side of the city, his eyes brightened. He was a lifelong West Sider. He said he had a mug club membership at a local brewery but had grown disenchanted with the place because although he'd been a loyal member for years, none of the staff had ever bothered to learn his name. They referred to him only by his mug number, 49. We invited him to stop in sometime to see what we were working on. He said he would. We shook hands and parted ways.

Several weeks later, in a rare bit of silence from the constant whirring of electric power tools, we heard a knock on the engine house door. I walked up to it, covered with paper for privacy, and peeled back the corner. It was Paul.

"Well, if it isn't number 49," I said, grinning as I opened the door.

He smiled.

"Just kidding, Paul. Come on in."

Paul stepped inside and looked at us curiously. "You remembered my name," he said.

"Of course," Max replied.

We had made a bit of a connection at the festival, and it wasn't as though we had so many business relationships that we couldn't keep them straight. He told us he was driving by and hoped to catch us working.

"Always," I said. We gave him the nickel tour, showing him the cobblestone stable floor on top of which we were going to build our brew house. We shared one of the bottled homebrews we kept there in a dust-covered mini-fridge. Paul enjoyed it and told us that when we opened up our mug club for membership, he'd like to join.

Months later, Paul kept his word and signed up. We were flattered and thanked him, but he thanked us instead and said that while it may not have seemed like a big deal that we remembered his name, it was important to him. We were touched. As a good-natured joke, we awarded him number 49. He canceled his other membership. Besides the engine house, Paul was one of our first strong links to the West Side. Seven years later, he now sits on our foundation board and is the esteemed holder of Mug Number One at the Mitten. Through the years, we've learned how friends like Paul can become instrumental in shaping a company's values, team members, and, most important, giving mission. Our long building process gave us many things, but this will always be one of my favorites.

A HUMBLE BEGINNING

Like the 2012 Major League Baseball season, our build-out began in the winter and concluded in the fall. We set our sights on a November opening, when we figured the work would finally be done. As we approached this milestone, the Detroit Tigers were chasing one of their own: their first playoff berth in years. This was a big deal in Michigan, and it even altered our company's history. When our licensing came through in early October, it became apparent the Tigers were likely going to play in the World Series. It seemed like fate for our baseball-themed brewery, and though we weren't exactly ready, we announced we would be open on October 25 for Game One of the 2012 World Series. That morning we were on the front page of the local newspaper, and customers began to line up outside an hour before we opened our doors. It felt too good to be true. But then the Tigers were promptly swept, we were met with mediocre reviews, we ran out of beer, and we were forced to close for nineteen days in order to brew enough to reopen.

Not the way we wanted it to go.

We were embarrassed by many aspects of our hurried opening, and I am still haunted by several terrible customer interactions in particular. I overheard one customer derisively describe us as exactly what we were: "a couple of home brewers who opened a brewery."

We were devastated. All the work we had done to outpace that very notion hadn't yet shown itself. There was no honeymoon period; we had to go back to work. We did our best to right the ship during the gap, and by the time we reopened, we made marked improvements in the products and the level of service. But although the taproom was full most of the time, we were acutely aware of our shortcomings. We knew that we were being propped up by the seemingly boundless enthusiasm for Michigan craft beer, and that it wouldn't last forever. If we wanted to do better, we had to invest in new processes, equipment, and, most important, people.

During those first few months, we were fortunate to hire many talented team members, some of whom are still with us today. We hired Megan Amante during our open interview day in September 2012. Our only applicant with any restaurant experience, Megan eventually became our friend, our front-of-house manager, and the host of the annual "Mitten Olympics." Robert "Wob" Wanhatalo was our original brewer and a large part of the reason so many people in the community gave us their business; to know him is to love him. Although he hung up his brewing boots after nearly a thousand brew days, Wob still helps us grow every day as an irreplaceable part of the outside sales team. Lyndsay Israel was our first general manager and, though she eventually became a high school teacher, still bartends for us during the summer. Jason Warnes was a tool-and-die worker and home-brewer who now serves as our head of brewing operations. Each of these people made our company special in some way, but none has been more impactful to our giving mission than Dana Mate Dones.

Dana started with us as a bartender, but she had experience in the nonprofit sector as well. She quickly became our resident crusader for equality. On more than one occasion, I watched her engage in spirited discussions (fights) with customers at the bar. I remember one time in particular when she was arguing politics with her own bar back during the Friday night rush. As I poured myself a beer, she grabbed him by the collar and yelled, "Not everyone can pull themselves up by their bootstraps!" Though much of her workplace conduct wasn't "professional" by any metric, we loved her. She was smart, opinionated, and always willing to fight for people who didn't have a voice. We wanted to make sure she stayed with us for the long haul, and we made her a part of the management team.

Dana now serves as our foundation president and is a tireless advocate for the disadvantaged in our community. She sits on multiple nonprofit boards and is responsible for fostering and maintaining our company's giving culture, an ever-growing challenge because we now employ more than a hundred employees at three locations during certain times of the year, a vast difference from our original staff of twelve.

OUR FIRST GIFT

Right away, Max and I found we were not prepared to run a restaurant. In our minds, we had built a brewery, but as soon as we opened, we realized the day-to-day operations were more like those of a traditional restaurant. We understood beer but weren't prepared for the reality that for so many of our customers, we're a pizzeria. On any given day, you'll see a lot of Diet Coke on the tables. This challenged Max and me greatly; our food service experience was the same as that of any high school kid who spends a summer in a restaurant kitchen.

Thankfully, our staff members were gracious and gave us the thing we needed most: their patience. They afforded us time to learn about our roles and forgave us when we made mistakes. They went through the journey with us and rarely quit along the way. Sometimes we were lucky and got things right the first time. One of these was to build giving into our plan from the start. We made our first company gift in December 2012. It wasn't as well organized, large, or effective as we wanted it to be, but we knew we had to start somewhere. Every journey starts with a single step, and each cause starts with an emotional connection. And this was a deep one.

For the better part of eight years, I had been a part-time caregiver for a boy named Nathan Hurwitz. Nate had been diagnosed with Duchenne's muscular dystrophy as an infant, but when I first met him in the third grade, the disease hadn't yet taken a very noticeable toll. He had some mobility issues but was able to walk mostly on his own when I became his classroom aide. Although he faced a daunting diagnosis, he was one of the sweetest people I'd ever met.

The school eliminated all non-essential aides (me) the following year, but Nate and I had become such good friends that his family hired me to work for them privately. I enjoyed my time with Nate, but it was heartbreaking to watch his physical faculties fail him over the next eight years. After he was unexpectedly admitted to the hospital for an internal infection, Nate's heart and lungs failed, and he tragically passed away at the age of sixteen in 2012, just weeks before the Mitten opened its doors. He had tested our newly poured wheelchair ramp only days prior.

My time with Nate both opened my heart and broke it. I had worked in special-needs classrooms for years but had never formed a bond as I did with him. He taught me that even in the face of our own impending mortality, there could be genuine positivity. Nate had his dark times, but he was rarely without a smile and never wanted to be treated differently than anyone else. He loved baseball and video games and was fortunate to have a loving family who took excellent care of him and saw that he wanted for nothing.

Nate's favorite song was George Harrison's "Here Comes the Sun," and his father asked me to perform it at their temple for Nate's funeral. Though I had dreaded it for days—unsure of whether I could even make it through the song without breaking down—I felt a strange surge of happiness course through me as I stepped up to the bema where Nate had read from the Torah at his bar mitzvah three years earlier. I strapped on my guitar, did the song fair justice, and stepped off the stage. Under my breath, as I walked down the aisle flanked by sobbing friends, family, and classmates, I thanked Nate for being there with me and, for one last time, reminding me to always look on the bright side. A few hours later at the interment, the thick clouds that had darkened the day since morning suddenly broke, and warm sunlight bathed Nate's close friends and family. We all thought of the song.

Before he passed away, Nate and his family had been raising money for the West Michigan Miracle League Field, a fully accessible baseball field in nearby Rockford that now bears his name. The cause made perfect sense for the Mitten, and we chose it as our first company donation. A gift of $590.10 to an enterprise with a total budget of more than $600,000 was how we inauspiciously launched the Mitten Brewing Company's charitable giving program. Although it was small, we had a feeling it was the start of something big. And we should know. The entire journey that got us to that point was based on the idea of doing a lot with a little. As it turned out, that would become the thing we did best.

CHAPTER 3

NON-ZERO

> "IT'S SUPPOSED TO BE HARD. IF IT WASN'T HARD, EVERY-
> ONE WOULD DO IT. THE HARD IS WHAT MAKES IT GREAT."
> — JIMMY DUGAN, *A LEAGUE OF THEIR OWN*

"BEFORE WE GET STARTED, I just want to tell you I think this is a bad idea."

Max and I looked at each other, dumbfounded. Our friend and financial mentor sat across the table from us, holding the first draft of our business plan in his hands. It was clear this meeting wouldn't go the way we expected it to.

"I have a grudge against the hospitality industry," he continued, sipping his coffee. As a CPA for hire, he had handled the books for a host of clients in different industries, including several restaurants. He knew from experience it was a tough business.

"Fair enough," I started. "But—"

"And in case you were planning to ask me, I'm not going to be an investor either."

The second punch landed even harder than the first. *Of course*, we had planned for him to invest. Max and I had all but counted the money. We were so confident he would be impressed by our plan that he would want to get in on the ground floor. Boy, were we wrong. The next hour wasn't very productive. We went through the document as planned, and though we did our best to digest his feedback, it was difficult for us to focus. He had taken the wind completely out of our sails. We were hoping for constructive criticism, and though we didn't realize it at the time, it was. His were legitimate concerns, after all. His critique showed us some of the obstacles we were up against in starting a restaurant, a pursuit that has destroyed many an entrepreneur.

Our friend was unimpressed with the thoroughness of our plan and felt the portion on giving was particularly incomplete. It wasn't that he thought it was a bad idea; rather, it was unclear where the money would come from. It wasn't reflected in the financial documents, and it seemed fiscally irresponsible in light of all the uncertainty we would no doubt encounter in starting a restaurant.

Yet Max and I knew we weren't starting just another restaurant. *It was more.* It was unique, community-minded, and inspired. But he didn't see it that way because it didn't jump off the pages of our plan. We knew then it was our job to change that, even if we weren't sure how to work our vision into a document full of market research and pro forma revenue projections. We did our best to flesh out our ideas, but our experience during the next few years taught us things we never could have known without actually doing them. Especially when it came to giving.

Conventional wisdom has always held that charitable giving is a zero-sum transaction. Whether it's money, time, or product, someone has to lose for the charity to win. And that's certainly true from the accountant's view: donations have to show up somewhere on the income statement, usually as a debit or an expense. But we didn't see it like that. We felt strongly that giving wasn't losing and set out to challenge that notion—even if we weren't exactly sure how to go about it.

BEER WITH BENEFITS

By constantly pursuing creative strategies and a deeper understanding of customer and staff values, we learned we could vastly increase the amount of money we were able to earn and contribute to our nonprofit partners, reaching totals greater than we could ever simply move from our bottom line to theirs. In 2018, we raised $52,000 for local organizations. In 2019, it was more than $75,000. Those are enormous amounts for a neighborhood brewery. The only way to achieve results like these is to make *giving a function of revenue, not of profits*. While it may seem financially counterintuitive, we found ways to regularly drive new business through our doors and vastly increase our capacity to both give and profit. But it took creativity, a deep personal commitment, and a willingness to let good ideas present themselves in their own time. Please permit me to jump forward a few years.

Our brewing team spent the winter of 2016 trying to develop an easy-drinking raspberry wheat ale. It seems like a simple concept, but, as any brewer knows, there's an inverse relationship between the easy drinkability of a beer and the effort it takes to make it. The lighter (in terms of flavor, color, and assertiveness) a beer is, the fewer flaws it can possess because there are no strong flavors to hide behind. An IPA (India pale ale) could be riddled with small faults, and most people wouldn't notice because of the explosive hop presence that defines the style. Craft enthusiasts can badmouth lite beer all they like, but the methods employed by companies such as

Anheuser-Busch InBev and MillerCoors to produce it don't come easy or cheap.

Raspberry also can be tricky to work with. It's more assertive than other fruits, so we can add less of it and still get strong flavors, but it's also very acidic. Too much of it makes the beer taste tart, and too little of it has customers complaining they can't taste the raspberries. It's a delicate balance, but getting it right is the difference between a customer asking for another and asking for the check.

As we brewed test batches of the beer, I began brainstorming names. Most of our creations have baseball-inspired monikers, and I wanted this beer to have a good one because we expected it to be a seasonal staple. So I went to the Internet. I came across a fascinating story about a former Negro League ballplayer from right here in Grand Rapids. His name was Ted Rasberry—like the fruit but spelled without the "p." New customers love to point out this spelling "error" on our beer menu, but I don't mind because it gives me the chance to tell the story. Of course, I leave out the fact that although I'm a baseball fanatic, I had never heard of Ted. But I knew I had found the name for our beer.

I made a trip down to the public library and microfiched every old newspaper article I could find about Ted. Surrounded by senior citizens researching their genealogies, I learned how Ted helped revive the Negro Leagues in the 1950s, organized the Grand Rapids Black Sox, racially integrated little league baseball locally, and even managed the legendary Leroy "Satchel" Paige. Paige was famous for his showmanship, which he would demonstrate by asking the infielders to sit down on the grass behind him as he effortlessly struck out the side. In the story I found, Satchel hadn't shown up for the game he was supposed to be pitching. Ted

Rasberry searched all over town, only to find him in the middle of Reeds Lake, fishing in a rowboat. He had completely lost track of time. Ted picked him up, and they made it to the game. Which Satchel won.

Ted passed away in 2001, but I wanted the family's blessing if at all possible. It seemed like the fair thing to do because we were hoping to capitalize on his name and legacy. After more than a few unreturned voicemails and emails, I finally was able to reach his nephew. When I explained my idea, I could sense some reticence.

"Well," he said, "Ted didn't drink. I'm not sure how he would feel being associated with alcohol."

My heart sank. I had read about that in an old article, and it was what I'd been afraid he'd say.

I had to convince the family this was a worthwhile pursuit and that a low-alcohol wheat beer was pretty harmless. So I kept researching. I learned Ted had a lifelong interest in giving to area children, even forming his own boys and girls club once upon a time. I began to imagine this beer as a vehicle to raise funds, perhaps for a cause like the ones Ted championed during his lifetime. It struck me as the perfect way to get the family interested and do some good in the process.

There was a small community baseball field here named after Ted, and I came across an article about its recent renovation and rededication, thanks to the fundraising efforts of the local YMCA and the West Michigan Whitecaps, the Detroit Tigers' minor league affiliate here in Grand Rapids. It turned out they were both administrators of the Inner-City Youth Baseball and Softball program, a free after-school activity designed to teach nearly sixteen hundred public school kids character, teamwork, and inclusion. Ted Rasberry Field was one of the fields they used.

And there it was. In light of Ted's legacy of helping children, it seemed like the perfect project to lend his name to. We set up a meeting with the sports director of the YMCA, where we learned the biggest annual need the program faced was underwriting for equipment (baseballs, softballs, bats, and jerseys). The budget was between $3,000 and $4,000. Max and I looked at each other and grinned. We were planning to produce approximately 3,500 pints of this raspberry beer in the first season. With this figure in mind, we settled on the idea of donating a dollar from each pint of Teddy Rasberry sold. We shared the idea with Ted's family, and they loved it.

The beer was fairly inexpensive to make, and its low cost put it in our Tier One pricing category ($4 per pint). But because it had a specialty ingredient and was seasonal, we knew we could sell it for $5 per pint without any objections. The donation was in each glass. In the spring of 2016, we released Teddy Rasberry Wheat Ale, and when it quickly became one of our fastest sellers, we were thrilled. We had created both a great new performer in our portfolio *and* an effective new fundraiser. Soon it became an effortless one as well. Fruit beers generally sell strongly, and although we took great pains to educate our customers about the program Teddy Rasberry supported, many of them happily drank it unaware.

We built the "Ted Rasberry Gift" into our business, and when April comes around, the excitement surrounding the beer and baseball's annual return ensures the program's needs will continue to be met, year after year. We use this *products with benefits* strategy often and confidently because we know our customers would rather donate to a good cause *and* have a great beer (or pizza or widget) than keep an extra dollar in their pocket. Markups like these are unlikely to raise any objections from the small business customer because *they aren't there to save money*. If they were, they probably wouldn't be there in the first place. After all, there's no shortage of cheap beer and pizza in our (and every) city. It can be tempting to want to use this strategy with low-selling items to boost sales, but this instantly reveals to our customers and team where the cause falls on our priority list. We've found it most effective to lean into what we do best. When we use our most popular items to benefit a cause, it shows we care about it enough to align our top performers with it. This has always produced better results than the opposite approach.

Before we knew it, summer was over, and we were standing on the field at Fifth Third Park (home of the Whitecaps), presenting a check for more than $3,000 to put gloves and bats in the hands of at-risk children who could not otherwise afford them. It was a rewarding moment, but it didn't come together easily. Indeed, both dead ends and ideological objections had to be overcome to make this effort effortless. But the good ones are worth it, and we've found that expediency only rarely leads to long-term success.

OLD < BOLD

Properly undertaken, giving is never actually a risk, and whatever we give always comes back to us in one way or another. But getting there isn't always easy, and it hinges on our willingness to stop viewing it as a liability or a repository for our leftovers. Giving is an active, evolving, and essential part of our companies and ourselves.

One thing I'm sure of: we wouldn't have $250,000 more in the bank if we hadn't donated it throughout the years. This was *new money* we were able to earn and pay forward because of our association with worthy local causes. Our nonprofit partnerships bolstered our company's reputation for excellence and generosity and led us to seven straight years of double-digit growth. The idea that "giving is losing" is defeatist, outdated, and just plain wrong. It serves only to restrict philanthropy's true potential. Why has charitable giving been stuck at 2 percent of the country's GDP since 1971 (Perry, 2013)? Because in nearly every article about business giving, one still encounters the same ideas from fifty years ago:

- *Give during the holidays.*
- *Donate for a tax write-off.*
- *Set out bins for old clothes.*
- *Host canned-food drives.*
- *Anything helps.*

These suggestions probably look familiar. None of them are necessarily bad, of course. But we now have a much greater understanding of consumer habits and preferences, so why haven't our practices changed? This type of giving won't grow a business and won't make philanthropy a permanent and meaningful part of its culture. Most important, it won't help nonprofits meet their goals.

It's easy to see why we're stuck. Even in good times, very few companies end their fiscal year with more cash than they know what to do with. And as sudden repairs, mounting costs, and expansion needs emerge when we least expect them (and they always do), what is the first part of the small business budget that gets redirected? "We'll be in a better position to give next year," one businessman might say. "Especially if we make *x* investment now." And that's certainly the "sensible" approach. As the proverb says, "Physician, heal thyself." But *giving is investment, not divestment.* And I set out to prove it.

ENTREPRENEURIAL GIVING

In February 2019, I took a survey of our customers. Although I had plenty of national data that showed how much consumers want businesses to support causes, I wanted to see for myself. Was the same true for our industry, in our city, in 2019? I asked ten questions. The results largely correlated with the national polls: our customers showed a clear affinity for patronizing businesses that support causes and vastly preferred local causes to non-local ones.

Yet I was most surprised by the response to question seven: "How much of your decision to visit the Mitten is due to our work in the community? Please select a number: one being the biggest factor and ten being the smallest." A clear majority—61.6 percent—of respondents selected a number between one and five. In other words, for more than half of our customers, our philanthropy was more of a factor than it wasn't. I was stunned. For the first time, I saw just how much giving has actually meant to our business. We knew we were outperforming industry growth trends year after year and that giving was likely a part of it, but we weren't sure how much so. The survey results were jaw dropping.

Not to sell ourselves short, but Max and I aren't restaurant geniuses. We have great pizza, but there's probably better. We have excellent beer and service, but there's probably better. I can assure you, there's more to it than business acumen. The survey also revealed how important customer *awareness* of our giving mission was. The people who responded in the six to ten range (the smallest factor) on question seven also responded similarly on the next question: "How *aware* are you of the Mitten's charitable giving?" If they indicated a small factor, they generally did the same on the previous question. This implies that probably *more* than 61.6

percent of our customers would care about our giving if they knew about it; we just hadn't done enough to reach them yet.

These results imply strongly that giving is anything but losing, despite the conventional view. But rejecting tradition is a key part of entrepreneurship. I constantly remind myself of all the people who told us starting our own company was too risky. How many times had we heard that we were making a mistake? How many stop signs did we run through because we trusted ourselves and our vision? But that's who we are, so why should we approach giving in any other way? Why be a gutsy risk taker when starting a business and then turn around and be traditional and conservative with the way we give? We must regard *all our work as entrepreneurial, including giving.*

JUMP OFF YOUR PLATFORM

For the giver, the act should be fun, rewarding, and as effortless as possible. Rebecca Laramee of the Sinai Health Foundation says that the key to connecting with younger donors comes down to four letters: MEGE ("make everyday giving effortless") (Fromm, 2018). Whether it's beer with benefits such as Teddy Rasberry or donations from pizza sales, we work hard to provide that experience for our customers and community partners, understanding that our platform gives us a unique advantage. It's pretty easy to ask people from most walks of life to eat pizza and drink beer. For many of our nonprofit partners, we are a welcome and fun change from selling high-priced gala tickets or asking for money outright.

"We can talk a blue streak about TNR (trap-neuter-rescue) and how we help community cats, but it really lends a great deal of credence to our work when others say it," said Carol Manos, the executive director of our long-time nonprofit partner Carol's Ferals. "It says, 'We feel this is a worthy cause.' When our work is seen as good and necessary by a thriving business in Grand Rapids, more people take it seriously. It's not just another crazy cat lady talking, it's a real shot in the arm, and it gives the impression of worthiness. And that is HUGE! No money can buy THAT!"

But a gift must actually be a gift. It has to be earnest, generous, and well informed. Nothing short of that will bring out the best in a partner. When Carol sees Dana's daughter Adeline running around in a cat costume, soliciting cash donations, or sees that Max and I brought our families down for event night, she gives us her best. A company must work hard to cultivate the type of energy that turns everyone in the place into an invested participant. Missing this mark ensures that our partners won't put forth their strongest effort, and our customers and staff won't be enthused by the results. This makes them less likely to give the next time around. We want each of our charity partners to become a lifelong ambassador for our company, and we encourage this by striving to be its best community partner. This is the difference between blending in with the pack and standing out from it, and, more important, it's the difference between raising a drop in the bucket and life-changing money. For either party.

Of course, not everyone has the fun atmosphere of a brewery to leverage. Yet every company has a place where philanthropy can take root. Identifying the products or the services that are the best places to give requires some serious study, but entrepreneurs are perfectly fitted to the task. They are uniquely suited to navigate the roadblocks that stop most people, and they are obsessed with finding new and better solutions to problems. Indeed, that's how most great businesses and ideas are born.

In the summer of 2018, as we stood on the field at Fifth Third Park for the second time, the stadium full of baseball fans erupted when they heard what we raised for the Inner-City Youth Baseball and Softball program. My thoughts drifted back to that meeting with our financial mentor. As I reflected on how in two summers we had created nearly $8,000 for this cause without taking a cent from our bottom line, I smiled. Unlike the field of play on which we stood, this was a circumstance where truly nobody lost.

CHAPTER 4

THE BIRTH OF ACTION

....

> "PLAYERS LIKE RULES. IF THEY DIDN'T HAVE ANY RULES,
> THEY WOULDN'T HAVE ANYTHING TO BREAK."
> — RAYMOND LEE WALLS, JR.

IT SEEMED A LITTLE too quiet downstairs. All morning, Max and I had been busy in our makeshift office on the second floor of the engine house, trying to make sense of the haphazardly stacked sales reports from the weekend. Yet we couldn't help but notice the lack of the usual din in the taproom below. I walked through the dry storage area, formerly the loft where hay bales for Engine Company No. 9's horses had been stacked, down the back stairs, and into the kitchen. There were no tickets on the rail. I looked at the clock: 12:30 p.m. Should be the lunch rush. Our cook John looked at me and shrugged. I walked into the taproom where Mallory, Dana's sister and our only daytime bartender at the time, was standing behind the bar. There were no dirty glasses on the wash side of the bar sink. No dishes in the bus tub. No tips in the jar.

"Have there been any customers today?" I asked.

"Not one," she said, frowning.

This had happened two Mondays in a row. I was starting to get worried. Though we had officially opened in November 2012, Max and I decided to close the restaurant on Mondays in order to catch up from the weekend and allow our beer another day to mature. We were selling beer much faster than we had anticipated and were forced to turn around brews in nine or ten days that should have conditioned for fourteen. We hated it. Cash flow versus reputation was the weekly battle, and it was agonizing.

In April 2013, we decided to err on the side of cash and open our doors seven days a week, but it hadn't been a good start, and I was scared. I began to wonder whether our strong opening had been a fluke, and the worst fears that can plague an entrepreneur were given oxygen: Is this thing tenable? Have we been fooling ourselves all along? Was this a temporary problem or a symptom of something greater? Was this just what we should expect from Mondays? We didn't know the right questions. But it turned out that giving was the answer.

....

As we learned firsthand, the perfect time for a business to start giving may be when it is struggling. While that might seem backward, the way giving organically evolves is instrumental in shaping a company, defining its values, and earning its customers' loyalty. Each gift presents its own lessons and perspective, all of which play a role in what we eventually become.

In our first year, most evenings saw at least a modest wait for a table. Though our beer and service weren't as good as they would eventually become, our pizza was widely acclaimed, and we rode the wave of Michigan's newfound thirst for craft beer. Our investors were especially happy to see that the taproom was always packed. That is, except for Mondays.

No matter what we did, Mondays were always a dud. Of course, this isn't unusual in hospitality. Restaurants typically struggle early in the week and often pursue *loss leader* strategies. "Open Mic Night" is always on a Monday or a Tuesday for a reason. As a longtime host of many such doomed endeavors, I was all too familiar with this problem. When I was performing music, I played to empty rooms all across the country, and I always wondered why the bar owners couldn't attract more guests. Now here I was on the other side of the bar without an answer. Life is funny.

What made the Monday problem even more vexing was how much better we did on Tuesdays. It just didn't make sense to us that we saw twice the business Mondays did, week after week. We were at a loss; since we were busy every other night, we hadn't even considered any strategies to fill the taproom. Our plan was simply to open the doors at the appointed time and do our best to keep up. But we had to do better on Mondays. Besides the obvious financial concerns, the staff was vocal about not wanting to be scheduled on Mondays, and the mood had become increasingly morose. It was starting to affect the service we provided for our already minimal Monday customers. We tried discounts and special offers, but nothing seemed to make an appreciable difference. So Max and I went back to our business plan for ideas.

In doing so, we were reminded of another shortfall: although we had made a handful of small donations, we didn't yet have a solid recurring plan to support investor nonprofits, as we'd promised. Living up to it always remained on our minds, but we spent every minute of every day trying to figure out just what in the hell we had gotten ourselves into. We decided to attack both issues at once by taking a page out of the well-worn restaurant playbook: we would host a Benefit Day. For one Monday a month, we would turn the restaurant into a fundraising vehicle for a local organization. We committed to donate 50 percent of the day's food sales to the charities our investors chose, and we crossed our fingers that this commitment to community would drive new business.

This was admittedly opportunistic, but we were also confronting an uncommon issue for a fledgling business: We couldn't fit in new customers on any other day. If we hoped to achieve the type of mutual benefit we envisioned, it didn't make sense to host a benefit another night of the week because the cause's supporters would likely just end up in the waiting room. We hoped to create a true win-win opportunity on Mondays. Over time, we learned new and better ways to go about it, but this was the only path we saw at the time.

Max and I came to this idea by studying how other area establishments hosted benefits, and though the framework was essentially the same, the commitment wasn't. Like us, most other bars and restaurants donated a portion of their sales on benefit nights, but it was usually only a small percentage and only for a certain number of hours. Often, a customer's money was applied toward the total only if that person brought in the requisite flier to prove he or she was there specifically for that cause. That bothered us. If we were going to benefit from these partnerships as we'd hoped, the least we could do was strive to be each group's *best* hospitality partner. We figured we could do that by giving more deeply and not discriminating against anyone who walked through the door.

Though it built slowly, this idea was the game changer we were looking for. It wasn't as rooted in purpose as we would have liked, but I always say a good plan today is better than the perfect plan tomorrow (apologies to General Patton). During the next few months, our confidence and business grew, any fears of losing money from giving were assuaged, and the possibilities of what we could actually accomplish started to appear.

POTENTIAL VS. SCARCITY

Though we would eventually form our own foundation, the Mitten's giving began in earnest by hosting these monthly fundraisers for area nonprofits. Our investors chose most of the early nonprofits, but we also worked in our own choices here and there. Our sales and the positive press affirmed that we were on to something, so much so that we weren't satisfied with the amount of money we were donating. We didn't feel that 50 percent of the sales from one day was impactful enough for our nonprofit partners. So we began supplementing the monthly event proceeds with a $1,000 base donation.

And I'll be honest: This one hurt, especially in the beginning. We could definitely feel it in the cash flow at the end of the month, and it was difficult not to think about the bills that could be paid with that cash. But I pushed to keep the practice going. "We shouldn't look at it as losing $1,000," I said, ad nauseam. "We should look at it as a time-sensitive motivator to make *at least* another $1,000 each month."

And so we did. We invested in better equipment and pursued staffing models that lowered wait times and allowed us to serve more customers. In our business—where there's a limited footprint and the tables are usually full—it's the only way to boost sales at peak times. And it worked. The extra money meant the world to our nonprofit partners, and they worked harder than ever to fill the taproom on event nights. Over time, these partnerships made our business stronger and more efficient overall. We knew this for certain when we noticed an increase in our daily averages across the board.

Rich Dad Poor Dad, Robert Kiyosaki's best-selling book on achieving financial independence, argues there are two ways to view the world: with a mind-set of *scarcity* or a mind-set of *abundance*. The former leads us to think, *I can't afford that*, and the latter, *How can I afford that?* Though I prefer "potential" to "abundance" because something exists only if we create it, *this viewpoint is absolutely essential for the entrepreneur*. Are we going to be satisfied with the revenue we're earning and seek only to acquire efficiencies, or will we repeatedly try to attract more customers? I find myself more in the latter camp. As an entrepreneur, I cannot be a passive observer in my business, and I cannot accept the status quo—in any respect.

ADVANTAGES

We soon found that compared to small nonprofits, we actually possessed some significant fundraising advantages. Not only were we able to use our wide social media base and fun atmosphere to encourage strong event participation, but we were also able to leverage all of the money we spend with our vendors. These advantages are best illustrated by our annual partnership with Feeding America.

In the summer of 2017, a social worker at our nearby public elementary school informed us that although the West Michigan chapter of Feeding America had been hosting mobile food pantries at West Side schools for years, its underwriting was about to run out, and Feeding America was unable to schedule any more until it secured more funding. He invited us to volunteer at a pantry to see what the organization was all about. One afternoon was all it took for us to realize there was significant food insecurity across every demographic in our neighborhood. When we saw firsthand how much these mobile pantries would be missed by West Siders in need, we knew we had to get involved.

The development team from Feeding America had a goal of funding twelve West Side trucks over the coming year, each supplying 5,000 pounds of food. We accepted the challenge. We knew our work was cut out for us because the project was far bigger than any we had taken on before, but our board was confident and settled on a golf outing as the vehicle to accomplish it. Though these outings are a bit of a trope in the nonprofit world, we felt we might have a competitive advantage because of our customer and vendor base. We were excited. The excitement wasn't shared by all, however.

Although they were grateful for our interest, the staff members at Feeding America were unenthused by the prospect of putting time and energy into a golf outing, and understandably so. Their experience had been that golf outings often required a lot of work and manpower and weren't usually very lucrative. In fact, they had raised less than $500—not even the cost to support one food pantry—at the last outing they had been involved with.

But we were bullish that our business relationships would enable us to secure enough sponsorships to meet our goal. We were energized by the organization's obvious and unique impact. While many, if not most, charity food banks focus on children, adults and seniors—two groups most forgotten about in the struggle to eliminate food insecurity—heavily relied on Feeding America pantries. The sad truth is that adults often are *hungrier* because they either forgo eating so that their children might eat instead, or they are too ashamed to seek or accept help. Sixty-three percent of senior households that Feeding America serves regularly have to make the painful choice between medical care and groceries (Feeding America, 2018). A visit to any of these pantries will illustrate these truths.

Max and I sent out letters to our biggest vendors, asking for support. A few days later, our beer distributor came in with a $1,000 sponsorship. Then came the same amount from our food supplier. And our T-shirt printer. And our insurance agent. And on and on. Our relationships had provided us with a major leg up, and before the first team even set foot on the golf course, we had already surpassed our goal.

On the morning of the event, we pulled the Feeding America development coordinator aside and showed him our napkin math. He hugged us on the putting green. At the end of the day when the raffle, the silent auction, and other proceeds were counted, we had raised enough to fund *fifteen months* of food pantries and were already accepting sponsorships for the following year on the 18th green. The next year, we raised more than $20,000 and ran out of holes to put golfers on.

Though this effort came together easily, it was only possible because we had spent five years working to be the best company we could be. We had done the work to be in a strong-enough position to ask and have people want to give. The act of supporting a worthy cause isn't enough; *we* still have to be very good at what *we* do if we want real outside participation. Attracting this is no different than seeking startup funding. People still invest in people, and we must be trustworthy stewards of our sponsors' commitments to continue to earn them through the years. I'm confident one of the main reasons our giving is where it is today is because of how hard we worked to improve the *business*.

WHAT CONNECTS US?

A lot of what we do has to do with *where we are*. Our supporters are the people who surround us, and because of this, entrepreneurs must also be explorers. We have to discover where our connections to our neighbors lie and how our emotions link them to us because we will constantly have to mine them for inspiration. They absolutely *must* be real and deep. Yet developing deep connections takes time and experience. The way we approached our first fundraisers was far from perfect, mostly because there was no particular target area or cause to which the company itself was committed, and the need to accept *any* nonprofit outweighed the impulse to select the *best* and most worthy nonprofit. Over time, this lack of focus would gnaw at us more and more, but in the beginning, we couldn't see the whole chessboard. We could only see one move ahead because we were just learning how to play.

Most of our early fundraisers weren't successful by our current standards, but our partners made strong efforts, and we gladly took our lumps as we learned. As they say, most of success is simply showing up. We kept our promise to our investors and triaged other causes as they came in, and boy, did they come in. We had created a monster. As soon as word got out that we were partnering with area nonprofits, there was a deluge of applications. It was clear that a significant public interest existed in what we were doing. Although we were overwhelmed by this, it had become more apparent that giving was indeed good for business. Event nights filled our taproom with new faces, each one a potential long-term customer to win over. We were starting to feel nearer to an answer to the question our financial mentor once posed to us:

How can you commit to something if you don't know
whether you can afford it?

GRAND DESIGN

The relationships with our early causes weren't as deep as they should have been. No disrespect to our investors, but these weren't *our* causes; they were *theirs*. Max and I knew that if we wanted our giving mission to grow and thrive, we had to develop the same conviction for it that we had for our business mission. We thought about what truly connected us to the neighborhood, and though it was rare in our 50/50 partnership, for once we completely agreed on what that was.

Most startups with deep pockets hire lawyers, architects, and contractors to guide them through the process. We could afford none of the above, so we had to figure it out ourselves. In the winter of 2012, months before we opened, we went exploring in our new neighborhood. Our talks with other businesses in the area pointed us to the City Development Center, where we learned that because alcohol production was considered a "change in use" for our real estate, we had to work with the city Planning Department to make our use meet the zoning standards. Planning encouraged us to seek the support of the local neighborhood organization before we went any further because if this group opposed our business, it was unlikely our idea would become a reality. And that was horrifying to prospective business owners, to learn their dream could be dashed with a single stroke of the Planning Commissioner's pen.

Max and I contacted the West Grand Neighborhood Organization (whose office was only two blocks away from the engine house) and told its members we'd like to discuss our intention to open a brewery. They invited us to attend their next public meeting, which, it turned out, also happened to be their Christmas gathering. When we walked into the "gathering" and saw that it was actually a cocktail party, one bustling with a veritable "who's who" of local business owners and politicians, we were nervous. Expecting a completely different atmosphere, I had prepared a very professional speech about our plans for the Mitten. I had even practiced it in front of the mirror. Yet it now seemed silly. As we looked around for anyone who appeared as if he or she might be in charge, a woman yelled out from across the room, "Hey! Are you the brewery guys?!"

A hush fell over the room, and everyone stared at us.

"Yes," we said meekly.

The woman then ran across the office, bear-hugged both of us, and tearfully whispered, "Thank you for doing this here." That woman was Nola Steketee, the executive director of WGNO, and as long as I live, I'll never forget that moment and how important it was. In an instant, we went from hat-in-hand to feeling wanted and welcome. We soon learned that Nola always radiated that kind of emotion and selflessness, and that night she galvanized our relationship with the West Side. We felt at home. But her support didn't end there. She spoke to neighbors on our behalf, pointed us toward property grants, and even showed up to our Planning Commission hearing to support us. It was overwhelming, and it bonded us to the organization for life. I'm proud to say that years later, I jumped at the chance to serve a term on its board.

Although Nola has since retired, her impact on the West Side is still apparent, and we think and speak of her often. She taught us never to underestimate the power of supporting things we believe in. No matter how insignificant it may seem to us, we often have no idea of the difference it can make to someone else. Nola had changed our lives. She had given us our first deep nonprofit connection.

UTILITY: MORE THAN A BILL

WGNO was instrumental in showing us the need for community giving in our neighborhood, even in unintentional ways. Although the organization ran programs for impoverished residents and seniors, it was, in fact, impoverished itself. It was always on the bubble of insolvency and relied on small grants and timely donations to stay afloat. This was disheartening to us, so in May 2013, Max and I chose WGNO to be one of the first non-investor nonprofits we benefited.

After the fundraiser, I called Nola to tell her we had raised $1,200 for the organization and would deliver the check the following week. She thanked us profusely but asked whether it was possible to bring it down sooner. She needed to pay the group's electric bill to prevent the service from being shut off. Max and I were floored. We had no idea how dire the circumstances really were. Though we were saddened, we felt some pride in knowing we had just given this vitally important organization the ability to continue to provide its services, as opposed to spending its time and energy raising funds just to keep the lights on. In other words, our help with *utilities* helped this organization increase its *utility*.

Utility is the measure of the effectiveness or usefulness of an action. It's a concept invoked often in the study of ethics and philanthropy. I was unfamiliar with the term before our charity work, but now I consider it almost daily. Through the years, we learned a lot about it and found that working with an efficient and well-connected organization is the best way to increase the utility of our work, especially in the short term.

Our neighborhood organization's main value to us has been in serving as a liaison between our money and groups that need it. And this is hugely important. In order to be good at giving, it's essential for businesses to understand their role in it. We have to be honest about our strengths and weaknesses. *We're not social workers.* Our company is primarily a vehicle to raise funds, and in most cases there are organizations far better equipped to appropriate them. We need their expertise, and they need our money. It's often as simple as that.

Seven years later, we still often work and interact with WGNO. Its ongoing role in helping us identify community partners and increase the effectiveness of our gifts is irreplaceable. Our relationship is a partnership in the truest sense of the word, and we've been a valuable asset for the organization well beyond that first fundraiser. We organized and hosted the inaugural West Grand Block Party, the largest fundraiser in the organization's history. We funded "Neighborhood Improvement Grants" that gave selected residents money to design and implement projects that benefited their blocks.

Yet it went beyond mere financial support. In addition to the board term I served, Max, Dana, and I have volunteered at countless outings and once even painted WGNO's storefront. We've all helped one another meet needs that we couldn't meet on our own, and we've always cherished the true reciprocity of our friendship. We'll never stop being grateful to WGNO for providing us with our first deep connection. Nola constantly gave to other people the way she gave to us, and she demonstrated daily that there are very few problems to which some form of giving isn't the answer.

CHAPTER 5

MISSION CONTROL

....

"THE WAY A TEAM PLAYS AS A WHOLE DETERMINES
ITS SUCCESS. YOU MAY HAVE THE GREATEST BUNCH OF
INDIVIDUAL STARS IN THE WORLD, BUT IF THEY DON'T
PLAY TOGETHER, THE CLUB WON'T BE WORTH A DIME."
— BABE RUTH

"WHAT ARE YOU DOING here today?" asked one of our prep cooks. "Isn't it your birthday?"

It was. I sat on the floor of our pizza kitchen, laying tile, and it was absolutely the last thing I wanted to be doing. But the alternative was grim.

It was the spring of 2014, and the Mitten was the busiest it had ever been. Although we were grateful, every day was a painful reminder of our capacity issues. Our production brewing facility across the street was nearly online, and we hoped our beer shortage would soon be solved, but the kitchen was another story. Max and I never imagined how successful the Mitten's pizza would become—that much was evident from the size of the kitchen we designed—and the attention we had paid to the back-of-house issues just wasn't enough. The team was hot, cramped, and overworked. We heard through the grapevine that mutiny wasn't far off.

Max and I knew what we had to do, but we were handcuffed by a number of factors. There was some room to expand the kitchen into an adjacent area being used for beer fermentation, but the ability to do so hinged on completion of the brewing facility across the street, and like pretty much every building project ever, that was months behind schedule. Getting permits was taking longer than expected, and we had a hard time finding a reliable (and affordable) HVAC contractor. But none of that mattered to the staff, nor should it have. It didn't make the view from their house any better.

We kept reassuring them that things were in motion, but it sure didn't look that way. Every now and then, a contractor would come in and measure something, but they hadn't seen much action beyond that. Rumblings of a walkout trickled up to us through the managers, and I grew nervous as we headed into another hot and busy weekend.

So I came in early on the morning of April 16; moved all the 2x4s, drywall tools, and other assorted junk out of the kitchen; and started mixing mortar. Tiling wasn't really the next step in the project, but it was the only one that I more or less knew how to do. When the morning crew walked in, I was dirty, sweaty, and standing over some of the worst tile work known to man. But it was *effort*, and the crew appreciated it. It meant more than words. After that, progress started to move more quickly, and, thankfully, the walk-out we were afraid of never materialized. Gestures matter. They demonstrate in very real ways that we're all in it together.

. . . .

Fidelity to a mission is a battle fought on two fronts, excepting sole proprietorships. For the rest of us, someone else has to keep evangelizing our values after we've gone home for the day. If I'm the only one who truly cares about the company's vision, I have to be prepared to work every minute of every day, speak with every customer, and attend every meeting until I die or the company does.

Even though our mission may be carried out in full or in part by others, it all flows from Max and me, and whether it fails or succeeds comes down to how good we are at making our team believe it. There's a well-known business graphic: "boss vs. leader." The *boss* is standing on top of a big block that's being pulled forward by his followers. On the heavy block is written the word *mission*. The *leader*, conversely, is in front of his followers, pulling the block along with them. This is *never* more important to understand than in a startup. Every day it's my job to *sell* the team on the idea that I'm the leader, not the boss.

In some capacity, we're all in sales. Even if it's not a product per se, all of us are selling something—in most cases, ourselves. I'm constantly selling the Mitten to our team members. I need to reinforce their decision to work for us and not somewhere else, and in that respect, I'm up against my competitors every day. Interestingly, this battle is rarely about compensation. Although our wages are competitive, most of this struggle is about *character*. When it comes to retaining employees in the hospitality field, fairness and ethics play a far bigger role than wages. It's been said that people don't quit jobs; they quit bosses; and when it comes to being the boss, authenticity is what counts most. Working in sales isn't sleight of hand; it's an earnest communication of value, benefit, and support. Inauthentic relationships turn invested employees into transactional ones, and this is a hefty price to pay.

For me, true leadership comes down to understanding the difference between *real power* and *position power*. The latter is merely the authority my position or job title gives me, which grants me *nothing* unless I deserve it. My customers and friends might care that I'm the owner, but my staff members won't unless they can see it for themselves. This is especially important in startups, considering they're often more difficult to manage than well-oiled, established businesses. The future is unpredictable, there is typically more stress and pain, and the staff is expected to work harder than usual until the business finds its footing. This is a lot to require of a team. It's essentially asking its members to share the burdens of ownership and none of the benefits. And when the job becomes taxing and the workload seems unreasonable, it's the person in charge who bears the scorn. Because of this, there's one style of leadership I've learned to value above all.

SERVE THE SERVANTS

True leadership is giving team members the tools they need to succeed. *They* want to succeed; *I* want them to succeed. If I work tirelessly to give them those means—whether it be a better product to sell, a better cause to support, or a better company that they can be proud to work for—they will meet our shared goals. If our beer and pizza are better, they become more exciting to sell. My staff can recommend them more freely and truthfully to customers and share in the rewards when people are satisfied. If a remarkable product also benefits a remarkable cause, even better. Authenticity and teamwork breed long-term success we can all be proud of. The way to best achieve this is through *Servant Leadership*.

In our business, it's the only style that makes sense. With three locations and more than four hundred seats to fill, Max and

I can be involved in only a handful of customer interactions a day, relative to the total. Most of our day is spent making sure the staff and the management have the tools they need to carry out the company's mission. There are times that require us to get in the trenches and work alongside them, but those occasions become rarer the older our company gets. We've come to terms with the fact that they know their jobs much better than we do, and sometimes when we jump in to help, we find we do more harm than good. I've been kicked out from behind the bar many a time for disrupting a bartender's modus operandi.

Yet it's tough sometimes. One of my biggest fears as the founding entrepreneur is being seen by the staff as an out-of-touch owner or a dilettante, but I know that to some extent, that's unavoidable. Most of our staff members today weren't there at the beginning to see the ungodly hours Max and I put in, and that's okay. At the end of the day, servant leadership is fundamentally about preparing others to succeed and stepping aside when that success is recognized.

Of course, not everything that's important to a workplace is *work*. In addition to providing staff support, we focus on employee events and strive to maintain a close-knit and well-rewarded team. Besides meeting the obvious need to blow off steam, employee-bonding opportunities outside work are invaluable for team building. This is an indispensable way an owner can demonstrate the company mission and give directly to employees.

Our staff is conversant (obsessed) with every nuance and quote from NBC's *The Office*. It's been suggested that I have a little of the main character, Michael Scott, in me. That distinction can be a compliment or an insult. Michael was both the show's protagonist and antagonist, and his antics were often childish. But his love for his employees couldn't be denied.

Michael would host an annual awards ceremony for the fictional Dunder Mifflin Paper Company staff called "the Dundies." We hold a similar annual event titled "the Mundies," or Mitten Dundies. It's a silly event with mock awards, dance numbers, and sketches about the staff, written by me and performed by the management team. It's quite ridiculous, but it's surprising to see the positive effect it has on staff morale, retention, and inclusion. As our team grows, it becomes harder and harder to work everyone into each sketch with a funny bit, but the payoff is also much bigger. I don't mind admitting that the two weeks leading up to the event amount to some of the hardest work I do all year. It's part of the way I serve my team.

This event has a very real effect on making the staff feel valued and loved, and if seeing the boss in a stupid costume in any way makes our company a better place to work, then I guess I have a little bit of Michael Scott in me after all.

CHARTING A COURSE

Of course, giving needs a mission, too. Ideally, it should overlap with the company mission to some extent, and for companies that value giving as a defining part of their business, there should eventually be only one mission. Over time, a mission becomes more philosophical and less operational, and this comes with its own set of challenges, especially as it relates to giving. Some companies employ diverse team members from different generations and backgrounds, and the causes the owners prefer may not necessarily resonate as such with the people they depend on. So how do we chart our own course based on what we know best and can most ably support? By understanding *value alignment*, what it means for giving, and how the source of our money plays into it.

Value alignment is *the degree to which an organization's values, mission, and goals are in lockstep with those of its staff and customers.* And it's extremely important to understand. The success of our giving has always mirrored the degree to which it was aligned with the values of our customers, staff, and nonprofit partners. We must always remember that our ability to give comes from them; it's a direct function of our success and continued growth, and because of this, they deserve a say in where the money goes. Though the entrepreneur may be used to leading, the success of a company's giving mission actually hinges on incorporating *others'* values into *the entrepreneur's* mission—at least, to some extent.

But this isn't as easy as it sounds. Ideological differences abound in any group of individuals, and achieving consensus can be a frustrating endeavor. Too often, we find ourselves pitted against those we have much in common with, and we've all experienced how small differences in values can become big disagreements. So how do we devise a unified strategy for giving? How do we justify saying yes or no to a particular cause? Is it a gut instinct? Is it first-come, first-served? Do we give special weight to a request when it comes from someone we know? Should nepotism ever exist in giving?

Most important, *who* should ultimately decide? Should it be a democratic vote? How about a decision based on objective merit, however we choose to define it? Maybe it should fall to the person who knows the most about it or at least has the loudest and strongest opinion? Should the owner's opinion trump all others?

These are but a few of the many questions that eventually require an answer, but they're ones often overlooked in giving—and it's a mistake. A company's business plan and organizational documents must clearly establish decision-making authority. Shouldn't we apply the same effort to the money we give away?

After all, what is the point of spending the time and effort to raise that money, only to hand it to the first person who asks for it?

It took us a while to understand this. As the years passed, we received more partner applications than we could ever accommodate, and we knew we owed it to the nonprofit community to put forth realistic expectations. It was agonizing to have to say *no* as often as we did, made worse by the fact that we never felt good or fully justified as to *why* we were doing so. The process was very informal; we usually just discussed options until there was a consensus or we deferred to whoever had the strongest feelings. Each time we made a choice, we all felt a little uncomfortable about how we had arrived at it. We needed to change that. Perhaps the main thing we learned from our first year of giving was that our staff and customers didn't engage with our mission nearly as much when we partnered with large national organizations. We felt the disconnect as well, so we made the decision to partner only with local organizations going forward. We further required these groups to be small enough that our modest monthly donation—usually between $2,000 and $4,000—would make a real and significant difference for them.

We felt good about these choices; they aligned better with our evolving values and made the job less daunting because many applicants didn't meet these requirements. We thought it would make our decisions easier, and it eventually did, but right as we prepared to move forward with this fresh start, we were caught flatfooted by one of our previous partners.

"I'm sorry," I told her. "We don't partner with national organizations."

"Sure you do," she said. "You did it last year with me. You said it was a success, and that you'd be happy to do it again next year."

"That's true," I said. "I mean, we don't do it anymore. We changed our criteria."

"But you said you'd do it again," she snapped. "We've been counting on this money. You never told us you changed your criteria."

My heart sank. It was true. We hadn't told anyone outside our team, and I never thought there might be overhanging commitments out there. I wracked my brain, trying to remember whether we had made any similar promises. I told her I was sorry and that we'd consider her group again, but we ultimately decided it was better to draw a line than to do something we didn't fully believe in. She was rightfully disappointed, and when I got home that night, there was a nasty note in my email inbox. I had mixed emotions. On one hand, I was upset because here we were, trying to do something good in the community in spite of the pain and stress it often caused, and even our partners were giving us grief. But I knew deep down that even the best intentions don't excuse unprofessional actions, and I was mostly just embarrassed. There's no way around it: Informing someone that his or her group doesn't have our support is tough, but it's even tougher when poor or lacking communication is added to the mix. It was a painful lesson.

The next day we publicly announced our new criteria and made certain it was prominently stated on all our giving correspondence. It turns out it's much easier to say no when we feel good about the reasons why. An ounce of prevention is indeed worth a pound of the cure.

Yet despite these efforts and their general effectiveness, there were still gray areas that required judgment calls. Does a national program that has a strong local presence still count as a national organization? We struggled with this. Some of our best work has been with groups like Feeding America. Once when we partnered with one of these local/national groups, a representative from an application we rejected called us out on it. "I thought you said you didn't partner with national organizations," the email read. I didn't know how to respond. Feeding America sent us, bar none, the most worthy of all the applications we had received that month. Should we have chosen a group we didn't believe in merely because it fit our criteria better than another organization did? Sometimes there was no easy answer.

One problem we continued to encounter through the years was the tragic fact that almost everyone had a friend or a family member who needed help with medical bills. Although it was heartbreaking, we decided to draw a hard line on that as well. That is, until tragedy conspired to make us break it.

NEED STRIKES ONE OF OUR OWN

We learned that although we can adopt all the rules, the mission statements, and the rigid philosophies imaginable, we also need to be prepared to put everything aside when it's warranted. And we did when our company had its first brush with tragedy.

In October 2014, we had the good fortune to hire one of our heroes. Alex is a well-respected brewer and a bit of a journeyman; he has brewed at the best establishments in the area and is a seasoned industry pro, by any measure. In the months prior, we noticed he had been coming into our taproom more and more often, and we were excited because we looked up to him. It's always flattering when brewers we respect come to our establishment and enjoy our beers; it's a bit of the "canary in the coal mine" dynamic. As our conversations with Alex grew more frequent, we learned that he was looking for a new opportunity. We were thrilled when he said he wanted to work for us, and we jumped at the chance to hire him.

Alex had left his last job because he wanted to find a better work/life balance. He was a talented musician and wanted to explore creative opportunities with more zeal. He was very up front about his desire for more employment freedom, and though this lack of structure wouldn't suit us now, it made a lot of sense at the time. We didn't actually need nor could we afford him full time, but we desperately wanted one thing that he offered: microbiology experience. Every brewery that's serious about improving its craft eventually requires a basic laboratory to evaluate the health and population of the yeast it uses to ferment its beer. We were exactly at that point. Our production brewery had just come online, and in addition to being a little intimidated by the scale, we were concerned about the cost of losing large batches due to microbiological mistakes. Alex was the perfect hire at the perfect time.

He worked for us for a year, and our beer improved markedly. There were times when Max and I struggled with his lack of availability, but, all in all, we were happy with the arrangement. Alex was, too, but the company was growing quickly during this time, and the need for another full-time brewer wasn't far off. Though we knew it was unlikely he'd say yes, we were planning to ask him to come on full time. Then the unthinkable happened.

In November 2015, Alex came to me with a time-off request. He had an opportunity to travel to Guatemala with some friends, but the catch was they were leaving in only nine days. I wasn't thrilled with the short notice, so I told him it was unlikely. Customers flock to our taproom during the holidays, and we always struggle to make and keep enough beer on tap. This was the case even before we opened our second location in 2016 and our third in 2018. Alex was a little dejected, but he understood. I slept on it and softened, as I usually do. I figured Max or I could always jump in and help the brewers if there was a real need, so I told Alex that he could go.

On the morning of December 1, I received an email from a mutual friend. Alex had been injured in a motorcycle accident in Guatemala. Although he was alive and conscious, his injuries were serious, and his family was airlifting him back to the United States for emergency spinal surgery. I passed along the information to our devastated staff, and we all hoped and prayed for the best.

An online fundraising campaign began immediately, as Alex's family was facing unknown but obviously stratospheric medical costs. Though the Mitten already had a nonprofit partner for December, we knew we had to hold a benefit for Alex. We never even considered how it didn't technically fit into our giving criteria. It didn't take long for the entire craft beer and music community to mobilize, and it was easy to see how loved and respected Alex was. There was so much enthusiasm for the benefit that Max and I grew concerned we wouldn't be able to fit everyone in the engine house.

On the day of the event, we spent the morning arranging the silent auction items and stocking the cooler for what was shaping up to be the busiest event we'd ever hosted. We made sure there was plenty of our pale English Mild Ale on hand. Alex helped me develop the beer before his accident, and we had enjoyed many a pint of it together. Max and I rebranded it "ALE-xander Atkin" for the night and donated the proceeds. As evening arrived and the taproom swelled with eager attendees, keg after keg was emptied.

Halfway through the benefit, Alex arrived in his wheelchair, and the guests surrounded him warmly. The love in the room was palpable. We've been full to capacity many a time in the past, but I've never seen it like that, before or since. Between our contribution, auction donations from businesses all throughout the country, and pro bono music performances from his friends, we raised more than $12,000. Other breweries throughout Michigan also organized their own benefits, and the donations continued to mount. Though the entire need wasn't and likely couldn't be met, the events certainly made a difference for Alex's family, who faced a life that had to be completely reimagined in light of his paralysis.

When confronted with the worst, a company is well served to be agile enough to be able to drop everything and do whatever it needs to do. Certainly, our staff would never have forgiven us if we hadn't helped Alex and his family because of some needlessly dogmatic adherence to a mission. It was the right thing to do and the right time to do it. Pure philosophies are too stringent for the ever-changing landscape of the small business. *I learned that we must always consider our mission statement to be a living document.*

BALANCING ACT

Ultimately, we have to find the best balance between the causes that need the most attention and the ones that resonate with our tribe. This is never a simple process. It always involves some degree of compromise, which often leaves nobody 100 percent happy. I struggle with it daily. I'm personally drawn to the mind-set of philanthropists such as Pete Singer, who champion the idea that the most ethical choice is the one that "uses high-quality evidence and careful reasoning to work out how to help others as much as possible" (Effective Altruism, 2016). His philosophy of Effective Altruism contends that global causes of extreme need take precedence over more familiar but less dire ones. But, of course, that's not where the Mitten ended up focusing its giving.

Our business thrives on the attributes of our unique and diverse community and team, and Max, Dana, and I wanted to inspire giving but not completely control it. While considering various philosophies, we ultimately steered our program to support the highest utility efforts *within* our neighborhood. We knew we could do more good there than anywhere else. We can never forget that our very existence is a result of community support, and our people were telling us by their disproportionate support of some fundraisers and not others that they wanted us to help our neighbors in need. So we listened. Our efforts may not necessarily mean the difference between life or death, but there is entirely too much suffering and abject poverty in our backyard, and that's what we have focused on improving. And we feel good about where we ended up. That isn't to say that this giving focus might not change or evolve over the years along with our people, but that's where we have set our sights for now.

I'm excited to see where our giving mission takes us next. Though Max and I may have first written it down in my garage in 2011, it would have been a pity if we hadn't let our team, neighbors, and partners inform it along the way. After all, it's as much their mission as it is ours. Most of the time, the best way we can support it is by supporting the team members who carry it out. Sometimes that may be inspiring new ideas, helping an injured friend, acting in a skit, or even laying tile on one's birthday. Each is an equally important way to show our team that we are indeed all in it together.

CHAPTER 6

BREAKING THROUGH

....

"YOU CAN'T TELL HOW MUCH SPIRIT A TEAM HAS
UNTIL IT STARTS LOSING."
— ROCKY COLAVITO

"JUST SO YOU KNOW, nobody even knows what this charity is about," our manager-on-duty told me. It was event night, and I was asking him to pump up the staff to raise as much as possible for that month's partner.

"But I posted about it in the employee group," I said, referring to the closed online forum for Mitten staff. He laughed wryly. He and I knew full well it had been buried by shift trades and time-off requests.

Logistical problems like these aside, I could feel that the enthusiasm for our program was waning. The last twenty months had been a blur of twenty different partners, and I was growing frustrated by how much work I had to do just to keep the staff minimally engaged. *Shouldn't the fact that it's charity be good enough?* I wondered. *Why was the team on event night only as strong as I was good at making its members care?* I couldn't believe that the "garbage in, garbage out" philosophy applied to giving, of all things. But it did. And it should.

Any endeavor worth pursuing is difficult. We've struggled with bad people, low participation, and poor partnerships all during our giving tenure. The key is recognizing whether a setback is just that or a *plateau*. One requires getting up off the mat and trying again, and the other demands we rethink our entire way of doing things.

While plateaus can be frustrating and discouraging, they expose critical weaknesses. They present opportunities for us to abandon failed approaches. They force us to refine missions. I've come to think of them as similar to the purging burn of a forest fire: devastating in the short term, but absolutely necessary for long-term survival.

EMPHASIZE THE GRANULAR

It was September 2015, and Max and I were excited to be in Denver. It wasn't because we didn't get out much, though that also was true. Rather, it was because we had never attended the Great American Beer Festival. After the growth the Mitten had enjoyed the previous year, we finally felt comfortable making the investment to send ourselves and our two head brewers to the conference. But as I walked into the Colorado Convention Center, filled with more than fifty thousand brewers and craft beer enthusiasts, that excitement quickly faded. I never felt more insignificant in my life.

The brewery archetype—burly men with long beards and monogrammed work shirts—was everywhere we looked. Each brewery had a similar roster of well-made beers. The graphic design of the ez-ups and tabletop displays blurred together in a depressing ode to groupthink; anthropomorphized hop cones were the rule, rather than the exception. Some people thrive in gatherings of like-minded individuals such as these. Not me. I was afraid for the future. The craft-brewing industry had always been defined by its counterculture attributes, but now it was apparent it had crossed into the mainstream. I worried that our solidarity might be our undoing, rather than our strength.

Like thousands of others, we spent the week pouring our beer and struggling to articulate why we were special. The entire eighteen-hour drive home, I scribbled furiously in my notepad, trying to find what that was. I had a hunch the answer was more important than we all thought. That year, the number of breweries in the United States had reached its all-time high, having doubled in the previous three years. Competition and slowing growth were coming for all of us. At some point during the long trip home, I realized that we weren't going to find what made us special in beer. Or image. Or equipment. Or anywhere new, for that matter. We were already doing it by giving. But it had to become an even bigger and better understood part of who we were.

....

I've always placed a high value on being honest about the ways we can improve, giving included. Call it an inferiority complex, if you will, but I have always found motivation in my failures. My many failures in music taught me that when I do something the same way for long enough, I'll come to a wall. And I came to a career-ending one in 2010. The brewing business had been a welcome change, but after our first two years, the enthusiasm for the giving program that had defined us began to wear off. We knew we had to find a way to better engage the staff members because, ultimately, they're the people our customers spend the most time with. They're the ones who drive it forward. If we don't have *their* hearts and minds, then we don't have much at all.

At the end of our first year of giving, I wrote a summary that leaned heavily on using the amount of money we raised to describe its success. It was an impressive number for a company our size, and I was proud. Our customers responded well when we released it, and it even got some national coverage. But eleven months later, when I sat down to write the year two summary, it read just like a carbon copy of the previous one; the causes weren't much different and neither was the dollar total. I was unenthused, and I suddenly realized why the staff members felt the way they did. So I put myself in their shoes. As a customer or an employee, what would I want to hear about most? What was the thing that would make me care?

Results.

I knew what I had to do. I contacted each of the previous year's partners to find out exactly what our donations had accomplished. Of course, we had a general idea, but I pushed them to link every dollar to the effect it had. The results were more powerful than I had imagined.

Instead of writing we raised $2,000 for Oasis of Hope, a free medical clinic across the street from us, I instead emphasized that:

- We provided medical visits and lab work for eighty uninsured and economically disadvantaged residents of the West Side of Grand Rapids. In addition:

- We sponsored fifty-six children for one day of Boys and Girls Club programming, which included sports, homework and reading support, art, music, character and leadership development, a snack, and a hot meal.

- We allowed Make-A-Wish Michigan to give Alyssa from Wayland—who is suffering from bone cancer— her wish for an all-expenses-paid trip to Hawaii.

- We enabled Comprehensive Therapy Center to train fifty-plus volunteers in therapy techniques, train their entire summer staff in CPR, sponsor a brain-injured child's weekly tutoring for two months, fund two speech therapy sessions for a child with a disability, and purchase fifty new books for the lending library.

- We allowed Crash's Landing to provide one month's worth of basic medical expenses and daily care for fifty-eight individual cats awaiting adoption.

- We gave eighteen economically disadvantaged students with severe cases of autism spectrum disorder the financial support needed to attend an entire year's worth of classroom outings with their peers.

- We helped create the Paws with a Cause assistance dog team of Mark and Pryce. Pryce is a golden retriever who, along with other specific tasks, was trained to retrieve the phone and open doors for Mark. Pryce's goal is to work together with Mark to increase his independence.

With this, I cracked the code. I shared the new summary with the staff, and they were in tears as they read what they had accomplished. I knew right away what we had done wrong: Without knowing it, we had disconnected our team members from the very intentional act of giving by emphasizing the money and *not what the money did*. The guests may have given the donations, but the staff gave them the reasons to do so. The staff members are why the cash changed hands.

Removing dollar totals altogether reminded me what we're actually doing here: *we're trying to make a difference*. Our team members and customers aren't moved to contribute to an organization's "general fund" but rather to actual projects. People. Cats. Trees. For all of our sakes, we need to put a face to each cause and a result to each dollar. When we do this, it changes our mind-set and provides significance to seemingly meaningless increments. And if we continue to do it right, we eventually don't even need to ask. When a company is a proven steward of worthy causes and works hard to communicate the need, worthiness, and timeliness for a gift, we've learned that our customers will give without being prompted. I love it when they ask us, "What's next?"

In 2015, the Grand Rapids Jaycees asked me to give a speech about leadership. The Jaycees are a national organization of young professionals who provide networking and community service opportunities for members. My speech culminated with the Mitten's giving story, and I shared the same year-two recap I had prepared for our staff and customers. As I described how our donation had given Comprehensive Therapy Center the ability to sponsor a brain-injured child's weekly tutoring for two months, I unexpectedly began to choke up. I paused but soon found there was no stopping it. All of my emotions and memories of my brother Josh, his struggles, and how much he had personally benefited from the team at CTC welled up inside me.

I thought about how hard the team members worked on their benefit nights and how many of the families whose lives they had affected came out to show their support. My voice shook, and the tears came. The emotion was contagious, and I heard sniffles in the audience. I skipped to the end and thanked them for listening. And as I stepped back from the podium, I realized the true emotional power of how we think and talk about the act of giving. Even though I knew all about these things because I had gathered the information myself, hearing them back, quantified like that, had such a profound emotional impact that everyone in the room felt it. I think we all forgot where we were for a moment.

There's no doubt that knowing the names of the people we helped and the cats we saved connects us with our donations in a unique and permanent way. We want to see ourselves in our gifts. It's human nature. Carol's Ferals named one of its cats after me, and one of our employees adopted it. And, well, they got me for life with that one. We can never underestimate the power of charisma and personal connection. Great organizations understand this. As it says in the Jaycee Creed, "Earth's greatest treasure lies in human personality, and service to humanity is the best work of life."

TOMORROW AND TOMORROW AND TOMORROW

Plateaus are inevitable. Company values change over time, and businesses evolve. Missions solidify. And when one aspect of the business doesn't evolve as quickly as others, it's hard not to notice. *But this is a good thing.* Just as we acquired efficiencies with our business over time, we did the same with giving. Plateaus are often borne from pain and embarrassment, but they increase our understanding of what we do. The more we understand, the more we can act with purpose and effectiveness. As the great psychoanalyst

Carl Jung said, "Until you make the unconscious conscious, it will direct your life, and you will call it fate."

Our early failures with our staff members were partly due to the lack of alignment between our values and theirs. We assumed the inherent virtue of helping a nonprofit would bring about full-throated support every time. We were wrong. We took it for granted that our mission would trickle down and that others would care about it as much as we did. Looking back at old photos of check presentations, I realize it appears more like the owners reveling in their ability to write a check than a team accomplishment. It isn't what we intended, of course, but it was more true than not. Since then, we've learned that giving our team more ownership over the process is probably the most important part of making it better.

Max and I had done a good job of making our initial twelve employees believe in the *company*, but the giving program felt slapped on, just another aspect of their crazy work week at a brand-new startup. It wasn't that they weren't enthusiastic about the idea because they were. But the job was new and often overwhelming, and Max and I hadn't done a good-enough job emphasizing how important it was to *us*. Business author Patrick M. Lencioni wrote that "Empty values statements create cynical and dispirited employees, alienate customers, and undermine managerial credibility" (Lencioni, 2002). And that's true. But these weren't empty values. They were principles we held deeply, but ones we spent too much time communicating to our investors and nonprofit partners and not enough time to our staff.

ON THE BUSINESS AND NOT JUST *IN* IT

Max and I were tired. We were working twelve- to sixteen-hour days, and most of our early mistakes had more to do with that than anything else. Of course, a lot of those hours weren't useful for anybody, and we eventually realized we were caught in the classic startup trap of becoming embroiled in the emergent, rather than the important. It's difficult to see the big picture when there are fires to put out everywhere, and it's easy to lose sight of a mission. As Vince Lombardi said, "Fatigue makes cowards of us all."

I didn't start to succeed on a higher level until I embraced my role as entrepreneur, as opposed to my official "position" of co-owner and founder. It was a challenge. *Entrepreneur* isn't a job title; there's no training for it. It's a term that describes someone who *has* a job title, and my title as "co-owner" is largely chronological and mostly signals who owns half the debt. But the entrepreneur is the person who can excite the team and grow the business. This was where I was best suited to be. A risk-taking mind-set is required to attack the job of giving with purpose and creativity. By fighting through plateaus with honesty and innovation, we were able to recognize our shortcomings. This is how we realized we needed to better involve our team.

The year-two giving summary was a good start, but we wanted our team members to be invested in the process and not just in the results. So we opened it up. We began sharing our successes, failures, and insights as these occurred. We introduced them to the people we helped. Dana brought in adoptable cats for them to pet and provided regular volunteer opportunities, including community cleanups, food pantries, and even Habitat for Humanity builds.

Sociologists teach us that familiarity breeds empathy, and the connections deepened accordingly. The progress was slow but noticeable, and the staff members began to get involved. They started showing up for events on their days off. They formed their own environmental sustainability team. They designed their own projects, my favorite of which was providing free pizza slices for those waiting in line at our mobile food pantries. Most humbling of all, many of them opted in for voluntary paycheck withdrawals to fund foundation projects.

We can never forget the pure, unequivocal joy that comes from giving. It's easy to do when we become consumed with our lives and work, but it's important to seek out experiences that remind us of it and how our connections to one another bring it out. It's the boss's job to bring these connections into the workplace, lest we suffer the cultural disconnect that big corporations experience when they focus only on maximizing returns. If nothing else, we should give simply to brighten our own outlook. When I handed a slice of hot pizza to a shivering woman who wistfully told me she hadn't had pizza in ten years, I knew I had just received an incredible gift. Moments like that give us the encouragement to push through tough times.

THE CAUSE IS STILL JUST, EVEN IF THE PEOPLE SOMETIMES AREN'T

Giving can be a messy endeavor, especially if you do it right. While shallow, do-gooder giving rarely exposes a business to the ugly side of it, neither does it afford the business any real benefits. Real giving involves getting your hands dirty and dealing with setbacks, which seem like a heavy cost for something that's supposed to benefit someone else. But Murphy's Law tells us things will go wrong even when we think they shouldn't, and well-organized projects crash and burn all the time. While working with many small nonprofits, one of the things we quickly learned is that an organization is often only as strong as its director or key person. This was painfully illustrated by one of our earliest partners.

This group had been extremely eager to work with us, but as the weeks passed and its fundraising night drew near, something seemed off. Emails and calls weren't being returned, and the organization hadn't been promoting the event as it had promised. I smelled blood. Lackluster promotion is the kiss of death for participation-based events like ours. On the morning of event day, we received a phone call from one of the group's staff members. The director had abruptly resigned and taken another job, and she was scrambling to figure things out. One thing was clear, though: no volunteers or staff would be available to work our event. I didn't know what to say. I felt bad for them, but I also felt myself growing angry. What should that really change about tonight's event? Didn't they still need the money? I couldn't believe that not a single person could be bothered to show up for an easy donation, especially after the group's members told us how much they needed it. But as my frustration nearly boiled over, a thought occurred to me:

"The cause is still just, even if the people sometimes aren't."

There's no doubt a nonprofit can be made stronger or weaker by the people who belong to it, but that doesn't have anything to do with the people who receive its services. Any animus we may develop toward an organization's people shouldn't stop us from seeing the value it provides. That sounds simple enough, but it's easy to find ourselves judging the worthiness of an organization by the people who carry out its mission. My first impulse was to say this group didn't deserve our money if its members weren't willing to put forth any effort. But, of course, that's ego, and it isn't right.

After the dust settled, we still donated half of the day's sales, as we had committed to do. They gladly accepted it, and although I kept my mouth shut, I was still hurt.

Over the years, I've grown a thicker skin because this was hardly an isolated incident. We've had more than a few partners who didn't rise to the occasion or perform as we thought they should have. But I've learned not to judge them too harshly because we've experienced the same thing with our own staff. Many times we worked hard to organize outings and volunteer opportunities that no one showed up for.

"The cause is still just, even if the people sometimes aren't."

Bikes often go missing on the West Side, and one morning a kitchen employee's bike disappeared from our rack. After reviewing the security footage, Max and I saw that the fourteen-year-old thieves matched the description of teenage suspects who had been stealing phones and bikes in our neighborhood for months. We spoke with the police, and they determined that the teens attended our neighborhood high school, the same one we had donated thousands to mere months earlier. We felt betrayed.

"The cause is still just, even if the people sometimes aren't."

In the summer of 2018, one of our longtime employees was senselessly attacked. Although our neighborhood had a decades-old rough reputation by some accounts, there had never been a serious act of violence on our property. That all changed when a mentally ill man assaulted one of our staff members with a metal pipe after a five-word exchange over cigarettes. The attack was bloody and horrifying and shook us to our very core. Max and I visited our employee in the hospital the next morning and were heartbroken by what we saw. We soon learned the assailant lived on our street. In light of all the work we had done for our neighbors, we were disgusted.

"The cause is still just, even if the people sometimes aren't."

Everyone needs to come to terms with it sooner or later. It's an important part of giving, albeit an ugly one.

SLOW DOWN

The no-show from our charity partner emphasized the limitations of the system we had in place; the pace of vetting a different nonprofit each month was too frenetic. There just wasn't enough time to make intelligent decisions. By the time we understood each group's mission and were able to properly educate the staff and the customers about it, it was already time to move on to the next one. It was a vicious cycle that led to some poorly informed partnerships. One of America's greatest and earliest philanthropists, John D. Rockefeller, came to a similar realization, although on a vastly different scale. After his first few years of largely impulse giving, he faced a crucial impasse. He noted the following in his 1909 memoirs.

"About the year 1890 I was still following the haphazard fashion of giving here and there as appeals presented themselves. I investigated as I could, and worked myself almost to a nervous breakdown," he wrote. "There was then forced upon me the necessity to organize and plan this department of our daily tasks on as distinct lines of progress as we did with our business affairs" (Gordon, 2017). It was an important awakening that altered his giving for the rest of his life.

We, too, realized we needed a better plan. The plateaus we encountered showed us we had to keep finding new and better ways to give. This meant slowing down the tempo and picking fewer, better partners. It's a natural principle that if left unchecked, all things in nature tend toward disorder and the lowest energy. Entropy always wins unless we fight it, so we fight it. And continue to fight it. And we're winning.

What we learned by overcoming plateaus shaped and improved our company in irreplaceable ways. It even changed the course of my career. While the trial-and-error process always made us better at what we were doing, the longing to build our own projects was too strong to ignore. I came to the realization that I wanted to define my professional life by giving. Though I wouldn't form our foundation until years later, this feeling was the seed from which it eventually grew. And like a forest fire, where only destructive heat can release seeds that would be otherwise trapped, our failures were the key to unlocking it.

GIVING IS GOOD
FOR BUSINESS

· · · · · · · · · · · · · · · ·

> "BASEBALL IS ABOUT TALENT, HARD WORK,
> AND STRATEGY. BUT AT THE DEEPEST LEVEL,
> IT'S ABOUT LOVE, INTEGRITY, AND RESPECT."
> — PAT GILLICK

IT WAS AN EVENING like any other. After Shannon and I wrestled the kids to sleep, I sat on the couch to check my email and saw a curious message among the usual detritus of junk. It was from a producer at CBS News. He was asking to film an episode of *60 Minutes* at the Mitten.

I frantically called Max. We both agreed that an appearance on national television would obviously be a boon for business, despite the fact they were asking us to close on a Saturday (our busiest day) to accommodate the shoot. We scheduled a call with the producer for the next day.

We spoke for fifteen minutes or so, mostly about the history of our building. The producer mentioned the episode would be a follow-up to one they had shot several months prior. The subject had been the 2016 presidential election, and they had filmed a discussion panel made up of seven Trump voters and seven Clinton voters, all Grand Rapidians. The panel moderator?

Oprah Winfrey.

Max and I looked at each other, and I casually asked the producer whether Oprah would be coming to our restaurant. He sidestepped nonchalantly, and it didn't feel appropriate to press for more information. So we did our best imitation of two laid-back guys for the rest of the call. He explained that the reason they wanted to revisit this topic was that despite their obvious differences, the panel members had stayed in touch with one another and maintained a political dialogue without hating one another. A rare phenomenon these days. Oprah and the producers had heard about this and decided to film a follow-up episode. I listened excitedly, but in the back of my mind, the question burned: Why us? Surely, there were bigger and better venues they could use. But we weren't about to look a gift horse in the mouth.

The producer asked us to send a diagram of our upstairs taproom to their production team. Five days later, he wrote back saying that regrettably, the vertical support beams in the engine house were a deal breaker for their camera crew. Cursed by nineteenth-century architecture. We were disappointed but thanked him for the opportunity and offered to host them for dinner and drinks after the shoot. We didn't hold our breath. Max and I were half-relieved we could enjoy our Saturday sales as expected. I did my best to put it out of my mind.

Three weeks later, I was leaving work for the day when one of our managers stopped me and said a man from CBS was upstairs, asking for me. I ran to the second floor and luckily was still in time to join him for a beer. We discussed the history of the Mitten and the West Side, and the conversation eventually found its way to our foundation and the work we've done in our community. He told me they were filming the episode the next day, and although they had found a more suitable location to shoot it, he was interested in bringing the cast and the crew to the Mitten afterward. I asked whether the guest of honor would be joining us as well.

"TBD," he said.

He asked that we hold tables for twenty-five or thirty guests to be arriving around 5 p.m. I coolly assured him it wouldn't be a problem, but I knew it was potentially a huge problem, especially if a certain celebrity guest didn't show up. Keeping six tables empty during a Saturday dinner hour represented the loss of thousands of dollars, hardly worth it for some crewmembers we didn't even know. But for whatever reason, it still felt like a risk worth taking. My father always told me to trust my "tummy meter." *(NOTE: Once you become a dad, you start to say things like "tummy" and "potty" to other adults in public like it's perfectly normal.)* I've learned that the only yardstick that means anything is one's gut, and my gut was telling me to take a chance. I reminded myself that this was the difference between the "I can't afford that" and the "*How* can I afford that?" mind-set. A visit from Oprah would be worth far more than half a day's lost income. I decided to roll the dice.

Max and I, along with our wives and Dana and Mallory, came down to the Mitten early the next afternoon. Together, we deep-cleaned the upstairs taproom, touched up paint, and carefully arranged the tables in advance of the Saturday crowds. The "reserved" signs we placed on them confused many of our guests because we do not nor have we ever taken reservations. But it was the only way to make it work. The tables had to be 100 percent available if and when the CBS party arrived, and that meant keeping them empty well in advance. Once a guest sat down, we couldn't ask the person to move. Not even for Oprah.

As the afternoon wore on and the taproom began to fill, I felt the pain as dozens of standing customers eyeballed the empty tables. I wondered whether we had made a mistake. After all, we didn't even know who was actually coming. Were we being unfair to our customers and staff by not seating other guests there? Would they understand if they knew what was at stake? The worst part was, we couldn't explain the reason to anyone: if it came true, it would cause a scene, and if it didn't, we'd look foolish.

As 5 p.m. came, the producer messaged to say that they were running behind, and 6 p.m. was a more realistic time of arrival. I groaned. If Oprah didn't show up now, we were really in trouble. The tables had sat empty for nearly three hours, and I was painfully aware of just how many customers were packed into the lobby below, waiting to be seated. This was a big opportunity, but we were still very much a small business.

Yet at 5:45, the producer wrote to say they were on the way, and the guest of honor was with them. *O* was in tow. I hurriedly informed the staff what was about to happen, and Max and I walked down the back steps to wait for our guests. As the cast members from the discussion panel trickled in, a conspicuous black SUV pulled into our alley, and Oprah and her two bodyguards stepped out.

"Hi, Oprah," I said, acutely aware of the absurdity of that statement.

"Welcome to the Mitten," Max said. "I hope you're hungry."

Oprah laughed and said she was starving because she hadn't eaten anything—"not even an egg"—in anticipation of our pizza, which she had heard so much about. She had saved all of her Weight Watchers points for us.

As Max and I walked into the taproom with the entourage, the guests stopped eating and stared. A customer locked eyes with me and mouthed, "Is that . . . ?" I nodded yes. Shannon took one look at Oprah and started crying out of pure happiness. We sat down with the CBS crew and raised a glass to the occasion: seven die-hard Republicans were breaking bread with seven liberal Democrats and one of the most recognized women in the world. It was unequivocal. Max and I took a minute to enjoy the fact that this group was gathering in a place we'd made, on tables we'd built, toasting with beers we'd created. Not bad for two guys who were brewing in their garage not that long ago.

News of her appearance spread quickly on social media, and news crews began to gather outside, but we didn't let them in. We didn't want to create a spectacle. CBS had obviously chosen us for a reason, and we had a hunch it was at least partly due to our small neighborhood ambiance. We decided this would be best remembered as a shared *experience*, one marked by its intimacy. We didn't need to exploit it; word would get out, no matter what we did.

And it was the right call. Oprah was relaxed and worked the room, stopping to shake hands or hug every guest. She told us how much she enjoyed the beer and pizza and happily posed for pictures. Before we knew it, it was over, and the CBS crewmembers were loaded up and headed for their hotels. Though it all happened so fast and came about so unexpectedly, the effects of her visit have been long-lasting. People request to sit in the "Oprah seat" weekly, and I'm asked about the experience in nearly every interview I do.

Through the years, we've been fortunate to host many other famous guests, and I believe wholeheartedly it's because of our track record as a strong and generous business. The CBS producer later told me he chose us for our outstanding reputation in the community, which was likely bolstered by our giving. The pace of entrepreneurship often prevents us from taking stock of our accomplishments, but once in a while something incredible happens and shows us we're on the right track. I have a feeling Oprah will be hard to top.

ATTRACTING TOP TALENT

Celebrity visits notwithstanding, giving has benefited our company culture in many other ways, perhaps none more important than the way it makes it easier for us to attract talented employees and keep them. As of 2018, the Mitten boasted a retention rate nearly *triple* that of the national hospitality average. Our employee surveys confirmed that an employer supporting causes is a huge factor in sustaining employment. On a scale of 1 to 10, 1 being the biggest factor and 10 being the smallest, the average response to the question "How important is it to work for a company that supports causes?" was 2.169. This mirrors national polling, and it makes sense. Consider this: Washing dishes and waiting tables are pretty much the same anywhere, but wouldn't we rather do it at a well-regarded establishment that values our contribution and offers the possibility to enrich our lives and the lives of others?

We realize the hospitality business isn't a long-term career for everyone, and for a lot of our staff, we are a stepping-stone to bigger and better things. And that's fine by us. We're the Whitecaps, not the Tigers. Max and I do everything we can to provide our team members with opportunities to grow in the jobs they have and move on when they're ready. Building a strong résumé is part of that, and they need only attend a foundation board meeting (open to all) to find countless ways to improve theirs. And it works. On more than one occasion, our strong reputation and social mission have helped our former employees land jobs in their desired fields. And that's what's ultimately best for the Mitten. Everyone has seen how quickly an employee who has stayed past his or her expiration date can become the company cancer.

No matter the industry, a business with strong values has a significant hiring advantage over its peers, as our employee surveys and the national data plainly indicate. Our culture has enabled us to hire employees of a caliber you might not expect to find in the restaurant business. I'd like to highlight one of the best.

LITA CYBULSKIS

Our general manager Lita is a talented woman with decades of experience in high-level hospitality. For years before she worked for us, she and her 85-year-old mother, Chesa, a Latvian immigrant and lifelong West Sider, had been Mitten Mug Club members, and our staff came to know them well. In late 2016, we were searching for a new kitchen manager and having a hard time finding *any* applicants, much less desirable ones. We knew Lita had been in the business for a long time, and Dana asked her whether she had any suggestions for candidates.

"Sure I do," she said. "Me."

We were shocked. We hadn't even considered her because she already had a well-paid restaurant GM job, and we knew we couldn't come close to matching her salary. Not to mention it was the kitchen manager position—not the GM—we were looking to fill.

"Don't worry about that," she said. "Let's just talk."

It turned out that Lita had admired our business for a long time and was impressed by what we had accomplished in our neighborhood, so much so that she was willing to take a significant pay cut to leave her position with a major restaurant chain and come work for us. Several months later, she became our general manager and an invaluable part of our company and its culture. She makes my life easier every day, and I'm extraordinarily grateful for her.

When good people want to work for us, it makes me want to be better for them. This is one of many lessons I learned from my father. On more than one occasion, he's shared his wisdom on the importance of being there for your team, even when you don't necessarily feel like it. "When confronting difficult times, I always try to remember there are more than seventy-five people who work for me," he'd say. "Their livelihood depends on me going into work every day, rested and ready to do the best job I can."

That stuck with me. It's a powerful message, and it's true. We can't allow ourselves to be consumed by the troubles we encounter in our jobs and lives. It only guarantees we'll remain stuck in them. This is extra important for the giving entrepreneur, who carries the responsibility not only for his employees but also for his nonprofit partners. As with any job, there are plenty of discouraging days when I feel lost, but knowing that people depend on me being at my best is the perfect prescription. An overarching sense of duty adds purpose to menial, day-to-day tasks. People like Lita can work anywhere they want, and I owe it to her and our staff to work as hard as I can to make sure it's with us. Even on bad days.

Understanding this has never been more important than now, when small business owners report that the single biggest challenge they encounter is a talent shortage. *A company's best resource will always be its human resource.* Happy and fulfilled employees not only make the owner's load easier to carry, but they also become a marketing arm that can reach far beyond what we're able to touch on our own. Our young staff members love to travel, and everywhere they go they bring stickers and beer and spread the gospel of Mitten. That sort of love is priceless.

OPEN NEW PATHWAYS

All of this amounts to the necessity of embracing new ideas about the role that leadership plays within a company. *Change is good.* Research scientists who study human cognition have determined conclusively that learning new skills is beneficial for the brain; it improves how our minds work and opens new pathways that enhance things such as job performance. This can be observed from the newest hire all the way up to the owner of the company. I pinpoint the moment we started to move from a second-tier player to being in the same discussion as the best breweries in the Midwest: it was the day our "30 Days to Better Beer" program began, and I'm positive that what I learned from giving made it possible.

In the summer of 2015, Max and I weren't happy with our beer. Neither were the brewers. It wasn't that it was bad; it just wasn't exciting, and we knew our equipment was at least partly to blame. The sort of quality we were searching for wasn't possible with the fermenters we had. Besides being made of food-grade plastic, instead of the preferred stainless steel, they lacked the temperature control necessary to prevent the type of fermentation flaws we encountered. And it was well past time to figure out a solution. Customers are forgiving of a new brewery's flaws in the beginning, but after a year or so, they expect you to get it together.

Drastic changes were in order, and Max and I needed to step back from the day-to-day tasks to find ways to make the changes happen on a budget. The brewers, who had been patiently waiting for us to make this a priority, eagerly helped us brainstorm all of the realistic ways we could improve our beer in thirty days. Max and I committed to get them done. We earmarked costs and put due dates on each item, leaving just enough room for payroll to clear and bills to be paid. It was hard and required serious financial sacrifice, but it worked. By the time the thirtieth day came around, most of the new equipment was installed and functional, and we could tell even before the beers reached the taps that they had made a noticeable leap in quality. We were so energized that we immediately started the next phase, called "30 More Days to Even Better Beer." Not very creative, I know. But we did it again and made another, albeit smaller leap, mostly because there was less to fix.

The staff was invigorated and loved seeing customer reactions to the new beers. We were happy but still not satisfied. There was no doubt that the beers were cleaner and better, but something was still missing. And I wasn't sure what came next. The sixty days of improvements had been a success, but we had reached the end of what we knew to do. Upgrading the equipment simply required finding the cash to spend, but the sensory aspects of what makes beer enjoyable proved more elusive. I knew we needed help from people outside our team—seasoned professionals, ideally—but we were out of money. Hiring a consultant or a new brewer wasn't an option, and other brewers are generally a little stingy about sharing their secrets. And then inspiration struck.

The last phase of the Better Beer program and certainly the most humbling of all was the "Industry Dinner." I handpicked the people I respected the most in the Michigan beer community— head brewers, certified cicerones (arguably, the beer industry equivalent of a wine sommelier), industry sales reps, and brewery owners from all over the state—and invited them to drink our beer and tell us what was wrong with it. I sent out invitations that said the following:

"Friends, tastemakers, and beer geeks: We'd like to ask for your help.

The Mitten has come a long way since our modest beginning in 2012, and we've spent the last two years reinvesting every penny we have earned back into our operation. It is our goal to constantly improve our product and be included in the same conversation with the great breweries and beer community (read: YOU) in Michigan and beyond.

With the addition of our brand new 20 BBL brewing system, hiring of experienced personnel, and adoption of improved standards and practices, our beer has improved dramatically in the last year. But we're not there yet. We want to represent the best in our market along with you and make the strongest beers we can possibly make. We're seeking honest and unbiased feedback, and it's our earnest desire to take your input seriously and use it to improve."

I sent out the invites and held my breath. I hoped it was a bold move that would not only improve our beer in a hurry but also earn the respect of our peers. And it did both: twenty-four of the twenty-five people I invited ended up attending, and the humility it took for us to ask for help was applauded by all. Best of all, the feedback was extraordinarily useful. Our guests provided us with information you just couldn't buy—from brewing secrets to raw material recommendations—and after we made the changes suggested by the attendees of the dinner, our beer finally completed the shift we had hoped for.

To this day, I believe that tasting to be our most successful and also most unorthodox business experiment to date, and it wouldn't have happened without what I'd learned from navigating our giving challenges. This was only a few months after we'd experienced our company's second-year philanthropy plateau, and the way we overcame that gave me the courage to try the same strategy in this pursuit. I knew I had to reach people, whether they were our own team members or our competitors, on a deeper level, and emotional connection and a shared sense of accomplishment were the keys. It was the only way I knew to make people care about something that didn't benefit them directly. I had to convince our guests that this pursuit would elevate all of us, and I knew from experience that I could best accomplish this by focusing on results that were granular, were relatable, and could be experienced firsthand. Our shared experience in making something better together bonded us in a unique and personal way. Transactional leadership would have failed here. Instead, this group came together to defeat the scarcity mind-set and prove that a rising tide indeed raises all ships. It was a once-in-a-lifetime evening, and the participants still visit us and remark about how much the beers have improved.

As a songwriter, I always considered myself a creative by trade, but when the Mitten first opened, that side of my brain went dark as the problem-solving side took over. Our early struggles were mostly related to capacity and undercapitalization—issues that were largely objective—but as we grew, the thing that challenged me the most was finding ways to stand out from the crowd. It took unlocking unconventional ideas such as the beer tasting dinner to get there. What giving gave me was the ability to *inspire*. Inviting our competition to tell us what we were doing wrong required a new pathway. Being limited by budget and expertise wasn't going to stop us from reaching our goals. To me, the success of the Better Beer Program is proof that when I acquire new skills by doing work outside my normal discipline, I'm likely to find ways to apply them to my daily habits.

DO NEWSWORTHY THINGS

The summer of 2019 was the best yet at our Northport location. Ten months out of the year, Northport is a sleepy town at the northernmost tip of Michigan's Leelanau Peninsula, but in July and August, the town swells with tourists, and local businesses are tasked with making their money for the entire year in eight scant weeks. Our fourth summer saw sales up almost 25 percent from the previous year, so we decided to pay it forward.

One of our bartenders was also a substitute teacher for a neighboring school district, and he made us aware of a growing student lunch debt problem there. Though it was located less than a mile from an affluent downtown resort area, Suttons Bay schools served a diverse population, thanks in part to a nearby Native American reservation. Many students there carry lunch debt, as well as the stigma and shame that come with it. Being a "lunch debt" kid can be tough. Not only do many districts provide these students with lower-quality meals than their debt-free peers, some even stamp notices on their arms that read, "I need lunch money." This angers educators like Joe. He and his wife, Jennifer, personally pay down some of the debt every year, as do many other teachers, but the issue persists.

The total debt at Suttons Bay was about $2,700—the perfect size for a Mitten Foundation project—so we made arrangements with the school to wipe it clean. Max, Dana, and I presented our giant check in front of the high school sign, snapped a picture, and posted it to our social media—as we had dozens of times before. We shook hands with the grateful superintendent and headed back home. We honestly didn't think much more would come of it.

The next day we received several press inquiries about our donation, and I did a quick phone interview with MLive, a large Michigan media group. Before we knew it, the resulting article had been shared online more than 138,000 times. It was everywhere. We received requests for comments from sources ranging from NPR to *Newsweek*. The Associated Press picked up the story, and it ran in major news outlets, including *USA Today*, the *Chicago Tribune*, the *Baltimore Sun*, the *San Francisco Chronicle*, and *US News & World Report*. As one online commenter wrote, it was "the cheapest advertising we (n)ever bought." We were happy but puzzled because it really wasn't unlike any of the other monthly donations we had made in the past. In fact, the $2,700 check paled in comparison to bigger donations, such as the $25,000 we raised at our annual golf outing. But it struck a chord. Lunch debt at schools had been an issue in the national press, with some districts punishing students for it and refusing help from outside sources. Plus, it was a few weeks before the school year started, and going back was on everyone's mind. It was a perfect storm.

Although viral coverage like this is impossible to predict or cultivate, the path to get there isn't. The more our giving is inseparable from our business, the more beneficial it becomes. The Ted Rasberry and school lunch gifts gave us more organic awareness than we could ever buy. Yet widespread awareness like this requires constant customer communication, something I consider the essence of *marketing*.

All businesses do some sort of marketing. Marketing is fundamentally about building relationships and communicating value to customers. It can be as low tech as engaging in face-to-face interactions. But since the advent of digital media and the twenty-four-hour news cycle, opportunities abound for those who recognize them. In my experience, *the best way to be in the news is to do newsworthy things.* Giving constantly provides us with a disproportionate amount of coverage, provided we find creative and engaging ways to go about it. Not only is this marketing free, but it also has the potential to be exponential. Each time we partner with another organization, we expand our media reach to include its coverage in addition to our own. This is an unbeatable win-win. We gain qualified exposure to new audiences in perpetuity and earn our way into the hearts of the cause's supporters at the same time.

This is nothing to sneeze at. It's difficult to make real connections like this with customers in traditional ways. Jon Taffer, hospitality expert and host of Spike TV's *Bar Rescue*, says it takes three flawless restaurant experiences for a customer to consider returning a fourth time, after which that person stands a high chance of becoming a regular (Restaurant Den, 2019). After two perfect experiences, there is a statistical likelihood of only 42 percent that a patron will return for a third. That's a frightening figure. Although we work hard to provide the best experience for our customers, things happen. Pizzas get burned. Ticket times run long. Humans get stressed. All of which reinforce the necessity of shoring up the company's reputation for giving and community service.

In this respect, modesty for modesty's sake doesn't make sense for us. For businesses like ours, whose ability to give is often based directly on a day's sales, some degree of "immodesty" is essential. We want to engender participation and enthusiasm, and we can't accomplish that without creating awareness. We never hesitate to share our good news because we know one of the best long-term investments we can make is to keep our business synonymous with conscientious giving. And it works. The week we made our gift in

Northport, sales were up more than $3,600, compared to the same week the previous year, far above what we had budgeted.

Time and time again, new customers tell me they heard about us because of the good things we do—and it's immensely gratifying. Since the beginning, we hoped our giving mission would make our community organically engaged and interested in what's next. And as I stepped behind the bar to pour a glass of the Stretch Golden Ale for Oprah Winfrey while news crews outside tried to fight their way in, I knew that this was exactly what we had accomplished.

CHAPTER 8

BUT IS ALL GIVING GOOD?

....

"BASEBALL IS LIKE CHURCH. MANY ATTEND,
FEW UNDERSTAND."

— LEO DUROCHER

BENEATH THE OVERPASS of US-131 and Leonard Street, less than a quarter mile from the Mitten Brewing Company, lives a small encampment of homeless people. Grand Rapids is home to nearly a thousand of them. The size of this particular group swells or shrinks depending on the time of year. Most of them are well known to our staff, and as winter arrives, this awareness produces action. Dana brings them hot pizza. Our bartender Lindsey donates hats, gloves, and scarves. Our head brewer Jason looks after one couple in particular; they struggle with drug addiction, and he buys food for their dog, Lady, out of his own pocket. Like many of the desperately poor in our community, they spend most of their days panhandling, and this underpass is notorious for it. When the light at Leonard and Scribner turns red, they take turns walking up and down the row of stopped cars, clutching hastily scrawled cardboard signs.

People like me sit there each morning with our left turn signals clicking, contemplating whether to give them money. And sometimes I do. Then I watch them walk two blocks to the liquor store on the corner and spend it on cheap booze. And though it upsets me, deep down, I really can't blame them. After all, wasn't I reasonably sure that was what would happen? And wasn't there a decent chance I would have just spent that money on a beer myself?

It's this tug-of-war between the heart and the brain that permeates the institution of charity around the globe, and this situation, with which we're all familiar, perfectly encapsulates it. We realize that by giving, we may be enabling substance abuse. We know the words on the cardboard signs are probably lies. But the impulse to give to people on the street persists. Why? *Because we can't deny it.* Our species survives because of our connection to one another, and in a world of complicated and rarely witnessed solutions, short-term relief bypasses the established systems and goes directly into the hands of the people who will benefit. This is powerful. We get to see it. Feel it. Experience it. It makes us feel good and assuages our guilt for having it better than them. And can we really fault a marginalized person for seeking some small measure of relief, however temporary?

Yet this compulsion to give creates divergent schools of thought. While it may be seen by most as a harmless act, many charities urge us not to give to the homeless. They say our kindness can kill, and it's often true. The world of philanthropy is rife with well-intentioned giving that arguably does more harm than good. Too often, resources are misappropriated, assets are overlooked, and entire communities are robbed of their dignity. All because people rarely challenge the outcomes of charity work.

WHEN GIVING TURNS TOXIC

Robert Lupton's book *Toxic Charity* scared me. It made me fear I
hadn't accomplished anything of value by giving. But that's not the
message to take from it.

The book, which is focused mainly on the world of missionary
work and service travel, critically examines the costs versus the
benefits of such efforts. Lupton argues that these expensive
mission trips can be more aptly described as *religious tourism*;
though they may be rewarding for the travelers, they often weaken
local economies and provide expensive, yet woefully inefficient,
"benefits." A Princeton University study concluded that the cost
of sending 1.6 million American church members on mission trips
in 2005 was $2.4 billion (Salmon, 2008), and although the true
financial impact of such work is difficult to determine, making an
economic argument for their usefulness is challenging. Lupton says
we encounter potential giving toxicity any time we approach it by
considering *our* needs before those of the ones we intend to help.
This is widespread in American philanthropy. We often see a lack
of material possessions and wealth as a call to swoop in and provide
them because we view most circumstances through our First
World lens. We assume that people in the Third World need to
have what we have to be happy. Yet we rarely consider whether our
actions might actually weaken those being served. *Toxic Charity's*
perspective is persuasive, well informed, and absolutely crucial to
understanding the full picture of charity work.

I struggled with these ideas. They rebuke much of what
has been the conventional wisdom about giving for generations:
that "everything helps." After I finished the book, I went back
through every charitable action we ever undertook and attempted
to determine whether each was helpful or harmful. I immediately

thought of our Habitat for Humanity outing. We spent the entire day painting a home for a local family, and although the coordinator did his best to be patient with us, I'm fairly certain their crew had to repaint most of it after we left. Was that volunteer day for *us* or for *that family*? Was spending a day supervising our sub-par work the best use of the charity's time and resources? I also asked myself: When we hand out food at mobile pantries, are we just creating dependency? Are we preventing these people from finding a way to buy their own? These are hard questions to ask and even harder ones to answer. But that's precisely the point. Lupton is telling us above all to become aware of the consequences of our actions and to remember that charity work doesn't get a free pass just because most people believe it's above reproach. He teaches us that the outcomes of giving should be examined just as critically as a business evaluates its bottom line.

Authors Steve Corbett and Brian Fikkert reached many of the same conclusions in *When Helping Hurts*. Particularly instructive is the book's framework for determining which giving actions are appropriate, which are not, and why. The authors identify three phases to resolving a crisis: *relief, rehabilitation*, and *development*. They define *relief* as "the urgent and temporary provision of emergency aid to reduce immediate suffering from a natural or man-made crisis." The other two phases should occur *only* after relief has been administered. Too often, charities default to relief work when rehabilitation or development is actually more appropriate. When we provide relief that isn't warranted, it's likely we create reliance and expectation, both of which make it harder for those we help to take personal responsibility for improving their lives.

But how do we know one phase from the other? Corbett and Fikkert say we can identify the need for relief by determining whether a crisis is *seldom*, *immediate*, and *temporary*. If all three are true, then relief is the appropriate action. If not, we move on to the other two. Philanthropists in the First World often miss this mark because of a deeply held sense of *paternalism*, or assuming that because of their material wealth and education, they know better than those in the majority or developing world. We must understand that not all work is relief, and sometimes giving can be as simple as amplifying an *existing* resource or asset. *Toxic Charity* shares how after Hurricane Mitch, U.S. missionaries descended on Honduras to rebuild homes at an average cost of $30,000 per home, even though the skilled laborers there could have built them for $3,000 each. Corbett and Fikkert recount a story of painting a house on a mission trip while several of the able-bodied occupants sat on the floor and watched them. Besides the economic absurdity involved, both incidents clearly robbed the intended beneficiaries of the pride in ownership that would have come with doing the work themselves. This practice is known as *one-way giving*, and it's easy to see it at work in many charitable actions.

PARTNERS, NOT BENEFACTORS

But what gives me the right to go to a food pantry and ask people in line how they got into this situation and whether it was their fault? Should we make it a habit to be suspicious of those who ask us for help? Should we assume all people in need can actually take care of all their problems themselves?

NO.

Of course, working for something is better than having it handed to us, *but employment does not necessarily equal affluence.* Though our biases about poverty may lead us to draw binary conclusions about it, the truth is much more ambiguous. The vast number of poor Americans do in fact work (59 percent of poor adults who are able to work, do (ATD Fourth World USA, 2018), and the gap between low wages and a high cost of living is often at the root of their poverty. When we add addiction, abuse, and disability to the equation, the lines between relief and rehabilitation become increasingly blurred. Unfortunately, our assumptions about what need looks like are powerful and long-held, almost as much as our impulse to give. This can be a dangerous combination.

In 2010, an entrepreneur in Florida had a big idea: he was going to collect a million T-shirts and send them to Africa to clothe the poor (Wadhams, 2010). But the idea—admirable on face value—attracted harsh criticism from well-schooled foreign aid workers. Before he knew it, the entrepreneur was the poster child for uninformed do-gooders. What happened? He neglected to determine the actual *need* for his idea. Critics were quick to point out that Africans, by and large, had no problems finding or owning clothing, and that the very idea that sharing T-shirts was "going to save the world" was naive and, more important, wrong. International aid workers who participated in relief efforts for the 2004 Asian tsunami and the 2010 Haiti earthquake were particularly critical, having experienced the problems that a glut of old, soiled, and essentially worthless items from well-intentioned U.S. donors can cause. Disposing of these unusable items creates a whole new set of challenges for those confronting an already overwhelming catastrophe. In addition, floods of free T-shirts entering the African market can actually make poverty worse by bankrupting local merchants who make a living by selling clothing. Entire textile industries in countries throughout Africa collapsed in the 1970s and the 1980s because of the effects of cheap imports.

So we see how easily a noble idea became a symbol of capitalist waste and hegemony, and I'd be remiss if I didn't admit we made mistakes in that same spirit. More than a few of our early projects were based on misguided notions. Thankfully, most never got off the ground, and the ones that did were soon forgotten. I recall one project in particular where we found out that most of our donation was spent on swag for bigger donors. Worse, we've even given money to partners who didn't really need or want it. Talk about paternalism in action. I suppose I'm just grateful our stage is much smaller. Although too often our failures are public and our successes private, mistakes like these are an important reminder to discard the idea that "everything helps" and focus on being an effective *partner*, not just a benefactor.

MOVING BEYOND WHAT FEELS GOOD

Similar to donating T-shirts to Africa, organizing a food drive and collecting canned goods certainly seem like good ideas. After all, most individuals have at least a few cans of food they'll never eat, and people are hungry everywhere. But anyone who works in a food bank tells us it's a waste of time and energy; what they really need is money.

The United States actually has a surplus of food, and nearly 40 percent of it goes to waste (NRDC Inc., 2010). This excess food can be acquired for little to no cost by national networks of food banks. For the same amount of money they'd spend on buying cans for a food drive, donors can feed twenty times more hungry people by providing cash instead. In a *Slate* magazine interview with Katherina Rosqueta of the University of Pennsylvania's Center for High Impact Philanthropy, the interviewer noted that Rosqueta "observes that a surprisingly large proportion of food—as much as

50 percent—provided to needy families in basic boxes winds up going uneaten. When you go to the grocery store, after all, you don't come home with a random assortment of stuff. You buy food that you like, that you know how to prepare, and that your family is willing to eat. A donation box with high-sodium soups could end up going to people with high blood pressure, and nuts could end up being donated to families with allergic kids. Social service providers know their clients better and, with cash in hand, can pull together items people are likely to want and let them pick what they need, cutting down on waste" (Yglesias, 2011).

This message has difficulty registering with donors because it seems cold, impersonal, and less rewarding than donating physical food. But this disconnect is responsible for unwanted food piling up and rotting in food banks across the country. An eye-opening observation by Rosqueta—that the world would be better served if donors placed checks inside empty food cans instead of giving the food itself—is an instructive example of how the actions that give us warm fuzzies aren't necessarily the best ones (Conan, 2011). This isn't just about food either; this lack of understanding may be at the root of a half-century of zero to lackluster giving growth in America. Our ideas about philanthropy haven't evolved nearly as much as the world has in the last fifty years, and bad practices remain ubiquitous because charities are reluctant to discourage participation or alienate their supporters in any way.

Worst of all, philanthropic endeavors such as canned food drives are often the *only* type of giving small businesses do. They are forever enshrined in the pantheon of a company being "active in its community." It's easy to see why; canned food is a tangible gift nearly anyone can make, it costs the business nothing to administer, and, most important to its institutional entrenchment, it makes the donors and the participants *feel good*. It's a powerful impulse, especially around the holidays, that's easy to give in to. I know this because we've done it ourselves, even when we should have known better.

One of our longtime partners is Kids' Food Basket, a community organization dedicated to fighting childhood hunger in our area. Its work in sending eight thousand children home from school with a nutritious sack supper each day is essential to local families in need (Kids' Food Basket, 2018). In November 2015, we went outside our normal fundraising model and challenged our staff and customers to fill boxes in our lobby with the items KFB needed the most: juice boxes, granola bars, and other healthy snacks. We offered discounts on beer for everyone who brought in an item. But after twenty days, we had only $60 worth of food, most of which Dana, Mallory, or I bought ourselves. The few items that *were* donated by customers weren't even what the organization asked for. We had no choice but to go back to our event night model, and thankfully, our customers came out in force as they always did. We took the money we raised to Costco and were able to fill multiple shopping carts.

The money was obviously much more impactful than the drive, and it was a turning point for us and our understanding of our platform. Our customers prefer to give *through* the business, rather than *to* it. They wanted to come to a brewery and eat pizza and drink beer for a good cause, not eat pizza and drink beer AND go to the store to buy something for a good cause. Adding one extra level of removal from that experience completely handicapped the effort. It had nothing to do with how generous our customers were or weren't; it was just an example of how we could best channel their money and desire to help. People tend to give through the lifestyle *they already have, not the one we think they should have.* Retail habits and travel patterns are difficult obstacles to overcome, and it's not the role of the small business to change them—just to understand them.

Make no mistake, there are plenty of worse things than poorly informed giving. But when it's the only type we do and it supplants better efforts, that's a serious opportunity cost. One key lesson we learned with our Mitten Foundation work was to listen closely to our nonprofit partners when they described their mission and daily challenges. What they desired most might not have been what we had expected or even hoped for, but at least when we gave with that in mind, we knew our money would go where it would do the most good.

Companies looking to make a real difference must reach beyond facile practices such as canned food drives (not to keep picking on them) and challenge themselves to do better and start with the ends, *not the means*, in mind. If our goal is to feed hungry people, we should speak with our local chapter of Feeding America —a well-informed group with significant economies of scale—and let its members tell us what the most effective strategy is. Odds are, it's to give them our *money* and trust that they know how to acquire and distribute food much better than we do. If our goal is merely to feel good, then by all means we should continue to put out the donation box. But remember that man cannot live on creamed corn alone. Indeed, who would want to?

MYTH-CONCEPTIONS ABOUND

There is another implacable, deeply rooted idea about nonprofits: that they should be lean and grateful for any help they can get, no matter how small.

Nonsense.

In his now famous 2013 Ted Talk, philanthropist Dan Pallotta elegantly dismantled the long-held notion that a charity's overhead is a measure of its worthiness. We encounter this misconception often. When our staff members engage customers about a particular nonprofit we are supporting, they sometimes hear the question: "What's the administrative overhead?" Customers are looking for a low number, and anything more than 10 percent raises an eyebrow. Nonprofits are aware of this sticking point and often preemptively share their overhead percentage on their marketing materials. It's a question designed to give a donor more information about how his or her dollars are being spent, and though it's an admirable impulse, the answers can be misleading and beg the question:

Would *any* charities be more effective if they had fewer resources?

Pallotta and his organization, Pallotta Teamworks, have been criticized for operating very much like a "for-profit" business by employing hundreds of paid staff members who earn high salaries relative to their counterparts in the nonprofit sphere (May, 2014). Yet even his critics must admit the money the organization has raised by hosting popular multi-day events is staggering. Its HIV/AIDS bike rides netted more than $236 million during their tenure, and its breast cancer walks brought in $333 million. Both figures represent the fastest and highest dollar amounts raised for those causes in history.

Would those events have been better served if they operated on a shoestring budget? I find it difficult to say yes. Perhaps the main reason for their success was the massive amount of paid advertising created by Pallotta's team of skilled, well-compensated employees. There are certainly many leaner groups fighting for the same causes, but I doubt there are any more impactful. Pallotta once said, "Want to know why nonprofit organizations aren't solving the world's big problems? Because that's not what we asked them to do. We asked them to keep their overhead and salaries low. So guess what they did?" This pithy bit of wisdom flies in the face of what we hold as true, but it strikes a nerve. I listened to Pallotta speak to a room of hundreds of fundraising professionals, and to say that the group was enthusiastic about his philosophy would be a staggering understatement.

We expect charities to be pure, to conform to our ideas of what they should be, even at the expense of executing their missions. In 2010, the Susan G. Komen Foundation attracted widespread criticism for filing trademark oppositions against other charities—mostly small ones—using the color pink and the words "for the cure" in their marketing (Lynch, 2010). Outrage ensued, and it was easy to see why; it smacks of big bullying little. Yet that's not really what happened. All of the overlapping marketing confused donors about where their money was actually going, and it was detrimental to Komen's financial mission of actually curing cancer. Not to mention it's a completely different standard than we would hold a for-profit business to. "We see it as responsible stewardship of our donors' funds," said Jonathan Blum, Komen's general counsel.

Ultimately, we have to understand that it's difficult to judge the worth of a nonprofit simply based on one impression or metric that may well exist for a very good reason. Whether people rail against overhead, size, or tactics, snap judgments serve only to perpetuate misconceptions and harden them like stone. We've found it's most effective to do our own research and provide our customers and staff with a clear and earnest description of what our donation will accomplish.

SO WHAT CAN WE DO?

Show up. Focus on outcomes. Endeavor to understand the ends that each effort truly accomplishes. Be honest. Meet people. Get dirty. Deepen connections. Learn more. Challenge assumptions. Understand that paternalism is very real. Invest in success and the conditions that create it. Remember that our vantage point often makes giving seem less complicated than it really is.

In order to truly give, our interests must be subordinate to those of the people we're trying to help. This can be difficult to determine conclusively, but it must always be our mind-set. With well-executed giving, there are always secondary benefits for the giver, of course, but we must recognize that any blatant inversion of this order is a signal our charity may be toxic.

Yet despite all this, *we can't be afraid to jump*. Feeling hopeless about the outlook of both causes and solutions is the worst thing that can happen. It's important to understand the drawbacks of poorly informed actions, but we can never let them harden our hearts and make us afraid to be charitable. Though the bad apples get all the ink, there are good people doing good work everywhere. Well-executed nonprofit work offers scale, efficiency, and expertise.

While it might sometimes be unclear who benefits the most from giving, one thing is actually certain: Giving *must* become a habit if it's destined to improve. Our philanthropy I.Q. rose after each gift we made, and weak actions ultimately gave way to strong ones. This was possible only because we kept showing up and doing the work. Really, there's no other way because the benefits of giving often don't appear when you expect them to.

In the spring of 2019, I took my children to Westside Outside, a community cleanup we helped organize. Since that event, they have organized several of their own neighborhood cleanups, along with their friends. Every time they walk by a piece of trash now, they pick it up. It's cute, and I love them for it, but there's something bigger going on there.

I know the doubts that plague many of us who do community work: Are we actually doing any good? There are plenty of reasons to doubt it. I noticed the indifference of our neighbors when we picked up trash from their yards. When we volunteer at the mobile food pantries the Mitten Foundation underwrites, we see indications that we're promoting dependency to some extent.

But.

My kids learned about community responsibility from Westside Outside and about helping strangers at food pantries. And now they demonstrate both daily.

Although it can be excruciatingly slow and difficult to quantify, each small kindness plants a seed that is capable of changing the way we act for the rest of our lives. And that's worth way more than what we can accomplish in a single day. Now each time I give money to someone under the overpass, I ask myself whether it's for me or them. I think it's a little of both, and that's okay. It doesn't divert real money from other causes, and it demonstrates kindness. If this type of giving makes me a better person and helping others becomes a habit in my life and the lives of my children as a result, then maybe all giving is good after all.

CHAPTER 9

IN ALL THINGS, BE EARNEST

....

"NO GAME IN THE WORLD IS AS TIDY AND
DRAMATICALLY NEAT AS BASEBALL, WITH CAUSE
AND EFFECT, CRIME AND PUNISHMENT, MOTIVE
AND RESULT, SO CLEANLY DEFINED."
— PAUL GALLICO

IT WAS AN HOUR or so before dinner rush when I walked into the pub for my after-shift beer, or "shifty." I noticed the servers were huddled by the server station comforting Rachel, one of our newer team members. The manager told me there had been a bad interaction with a customer the previous night, and Rachel was still upset by it. I pulled Rachel aside, and she told me a family had brought their elderly father in for dinner. My face burned with anger as she described how the man sexually harassed her repeatedly during their meal, even touching her inappropriately on one occasion. Rachel was visibly bothered through the entire interaction, and the man's daughter explained that he was in the early stages of dementia and encouraged Rachel not to take it personally. Rachel tried her best to be patient, but as his behavior grew more aggressive, she felt compelled to speak up.

She told the family he was being inappropriate and that if the behavior continued, she was going to get the manager.

The daughter laughed. "You're in the *service industry*," she snarled. "You need to get used to this kind of thing."

They asked for their bill and left. Rachel cleared the table and noticed that not only had the group left no tip on an $83.17 tab, but they had also written, "Change your attitude!" on the check. Though she was hardly a confrontational person, Rachel walked outside and demanded an explanation from the guests. The daughter swore at Rachel and insulted her appearance, and Rachel came back inside in tears. Soon afterward, our manager fielded an angry phone call from the patrons, complaining about their dining experience. The manager apologized—unaware of what had actually occurred—took down their address and dropped a gift card in the mail. The incident was soon swallowed up in the chaos of a busy Wednesday night.

But the next day Rachel was still upset, and so was the rest of the female staff. I felt guilty because to some extent I knew I was responsible. I was all too aware of the times in the past when I had turned an indifferent eye to this sort of thing. Patrons demeaning servers has been a part of restaurant culture for too long, largely because the people in charge (me) accept it as a cost of doing business. Most women in the service industry become numb to it or skilled at playing it off, but there's usually real pain not far beneath the surface. I realized it was well past time for a gesture.

I found the customer's address on a crumpled-up piece of receipt paper in the office trashcan and wrote her a letter. I explained that her conduct was unacceptable, and although the gift card we'd promised had already been mailed, we wouldn't be honoring it. Her patronage didn't give her the right to demean our employees, and she wasn't welcome in the restaurant ever again. I sent Rachel a copy of the letter, and I shared it with the staff as well. I posted the customer's name and photo and asked the staff to inform a manager if she ever set foot in the restaurant again.

Though the damage couldn't be undone, I learned it's never too late to make a positive change. The staff members were understanding when I apologized for not doing a better job in the past, and they were quick to forgive me. The experience taught me something about leadership that I didn't know: Humility is one of the biggest gifts I can give my team. It breaks down the wall between boss and employee and shows that everyone has a role to play in shaping the company. Admitting mistakes isn't weakness; it communicates authenticity, builds trust, and, most of all, demonstrates that transparency isn't just for customers. Our team deserves at least the same degree of respect, honesty, and engagement that we afford strangers who walk through the door, and it's important for me to acknowledge that the customer isn't always right. Sometimes the customer is a jerk, and our employees have to know I'll defend them when it's necessary. They'll never truly believe in a company that doesn't do right by them. And how can I ever expect them to help *me* give if I don't give first and foremost to them?

FAIR BALL

Today's concerns often seem frivolous to older generations. In *The Affluent Society,* economist John Kenneth Galbraith argued that after World War II, traditional economic theories were no longer suitable. Most Americans now have their basic needs met, and to some degree our demands have shifted from basic goods to luxury goods. This demand is inorganic; it stems not from need but from *want*, and thus these luxury "goods" are often not goods at all but psychological desires. Research from psychologists such as Matthew Lieberman of UCLA indicates that traditional models of predicting human behavior—for example, Maslow's Hierarchy of Needs—may be less accurate than once thought because they underestimate the importance of social needs. Yet these needs are anything but frivolous. They largely govern our behavior, especially in the workplace.

Ask any small business owners what the most important facet of success is, and they'll say it's *service*. Always has been and always will be. But I'm not sure that's true anymore, at least in the way we tend to think about it. It still matters, but the problem is that great service doesn't really *demonstrate* anything. It's expected. There's an old restaurant adage that a satisfied customer will tell five people about his or her experience, and an unsatisfied one will tell twenty-five. Bad service is the outlier; it confounds expectations and angers us.

There's now compelling evidence to suggest *fairness* is what matters most, in both the workplace and the marketplace. Of course, fairness is a component of service, and there's an interesting phenomena that showcases how the two intersect: studies suggest that quickly and properly handling a customer complaint can actually have a *bigger effect* on repeat business than merely providing a flawless experience (Huang, Mitchell, Dibner, Ruttenberg, and Tripp, 2018). This is a difficult concept for most hospitality veterans to digest, but it makes sense. Screwing up and fixing it actually demonstrate this fairness we esteem so highly. It proves a company is willing to go above and beyond what's expected to provide an outstanding—not merely "problem-free"—customer experience.

Though we may just now be starting to understand its effect on our social systems, the desire for fairness and inclusion is primal, according to Lieberman. Mammals developed this link because social connection to those who cared for them was essential to survival. Today, it plays the same role in the workplace. Fairness is no longer considered the mark of a great company; its absence is conspicuous and often prevents companies from achieving their full potential by limiting meaningful employee contributions. The perception of unfairness triggers a threat response in the brain that can be as painful as a "blow to the head," according to David Rock, founding president of NeuroLeadership Institute (Rock, 2009). Constantly encountering these threat responses uses up resources in the brain in a zero-sum way. Fear limits our ability to think critically and solve problems, and pressuring employees to be better at their jobs can actually make them far worse. This hurts companies in ways they may not outwardly recognize. When employees encounter unfairness, they may suck it up and not say anything, but they reduce their commitment. Unfair work environments turn invested team members into merely transactional ones. They'll still show up on time and collect a check, but they'll save their good ideas for someone else.

Interestingly, fairness is rarely about compensation. Although still widely practiced, the tactic of using a pay raise to gloss over unfair treatment usually doesn't work because the desire for equity actually outweighs that of monetary reward. A well-known psychological experiment demonstrated this: participants who received 50 cents from a dollar split reacted more positively to that than to receiving $8 out of a $25 "split" (Tabibnia, Satpute, and Lieberman, 2008). The value of the received sum mattered far less than the perceived inequity. Economic incentives *have* to be paired with fairness and social advance to have any sort of motivational result because our brains primarily experience the workplace as a social system, one that thrives on the type of fairness that only those at the top can provide. In other words, the people in charge now have to *give* to their team in ways they didn't before.

And, of course, Max and I haven't always gotten it right. We've played favorites, made embarrassing mistakes, and been slow to recognize changing conventions. We've always attempted to be fair, but sometimes things ended up lopsided. Fortunately, we've been honest about our shortcomings and allowed our staff and customers to be heard. Even about the little things.

THE FINAL STRAW

"Excuse me, but you forgot to give us water," the woman at table nine said to her server, Hilary. Like many restaurant customers, she possessed the expectation that water is always served with a meal. But Hilary hadn't forgotten. It was by design.

As a brewery, we use *a lot* of water. It takes water to make beer, of course, but it takes even more to cool it down after it boils and to clean all the equipment involved. Breweries have become increasingly conscious of their water use and have adopted methods of conserving and reclaiming it. Customers applaud the effort on the brewing side but not necessarily in the dining room. Most people still order water by habit, though they rarely drink more than a sip and usually leave a full glass on the table. After witnessing just how much we poured down the drain each day, our sustainability team asked our servers to serve water only if a customer asked for it, and if they did, to serve it in 10-ounce water glasses instead of the standard pint. Hilary filled the customer one of these and brought it to her table.

The woman stared at the small glass before her. "There's no straw," she said with a sigh.

"Yes," Hilary said. "About that . . ."

Thanks again to the influence of our sustainability team, we had just discontinued the use of straws. We kept some on hand for customers who required special accommodations, but we no longer used plastic straws in our business, and they were on their way to becoming a thing of the past altogether.

After nearly seventy years of widespread use throughout the world, plastic straws fell out of favor with American hospitality in 2018. *"Utensil non grata,"* said the *Wall Street Journal* (Ramey and Tita, 2018). And for good reason. They're too small to be recycled, they don't break down in landfills, and they're *everywhere;* some estimates say Americans alone use 500 million daily. The movement to ban straws and other single-use plastics had been slowly gaining steam, but when a video of a sea turtle with a plastic straw being removed from its nose went viral in the summer of 2018, it reached its tipping point. Cities such as Seattle and even entire states—for example, California—pledged to ban their use. Corporate giants Starbucks and Disney vowed the same. Locally, restaurants and breweries announced their straw bans on social media, and before long, our staff was pressuring us to follow suit.

Activists rejoiced at the victory against this high-profile single-use plastic, but it wasn't unanimous. Critics were quick to point out that straws account for less than one quarter of 1 percent of the plastic waste in our oceans. They condemned straw activism as being a mile wide and an inch deep and warned it might distract from more useful efforts to ban plastics. Plus, the bans affected the disability community in very real ways (Vallely, 2019). And all of this is true. Banning plastic straws *is* obviously a very small and flawed step.

Yet what's most notable about the bans are the avenues through which they arrived. This ban didn't happen because companies suddenly recognized a harmful practice. It was the tail wagging the dog. For us, the tail comprised our own young team members. They made it happen, right down to sourcing paper straws and developing a customer-education plan. I'm not sure something like this would have happened twenty years ago. Joined with like-minded others across the country, our staff members set out to reverse a nearly century-old consumer habit in the span of one summer. By many metrics, they did it—and they didn't need an employee resource group or suggestion box to get started. They simply got together to find ways to see their interests reflected in the way their workplace did business.

It's easy to see how industry's influence on the marketplace is shrinking. Gone are the days of corporations being able to use their power and influence to control customer attitudes. Our team members are prepared to speak up for what they want, and with their mastery of the digital platform, they possess the most powerful megaphone of all time. This alone gives them the ability to shape our business faster than we can. Though we're privately held, these groups are very much our stakeholders. When they weigh in, we must listen. And if we pay close-enough attention, we'll see we can learn a lot about the future of our companies from the fate of the lowly straw.

OUR DOLLAR SHOUTS WHILE OUR OPINION WHISPERS

Economist and sociologist Thorstein Veblen coined the phrase *conspicuous consumption* in the late nineteenth century to describe the way the nouveau riche in America showed off their social status and capitalist gains. They consumed expensive goods and made extravagant displays solely to demonstrate their wealth. Today's youth also tend to identify themselves by what they consume, but in a much less craven way. As we can see from phenomena like the straw bans, conspicuous consumption still very much exists but has evolved into a less superficial, more socially beneficial practice.

Why was the straw ban so important to our staff? It didn't benefit them financially; likely the opposite, in fact. Our sustainability team is volunteer-led, and the ban caused confusion and friction with customers more than a few times. It's because the ban allowed our staff members to demonstrate their impact on the social system in which they work. In a 2017 Ford Motor Company study on consumer behavior, the majority of individuals surveyed consider prosperity as being less about wealth and more about happiness and personal fulfillment (Ford Motor Company, 2018). This represents a major shift in what it means to "live the good life," and many of us now place more value on pursuing meaningful experiences than on achieving material success. It's important to find ways for our team members to shape the way we do business, even if it's outside their job description. If not, they'll find someplace else where they can. But what about the consumer space? If fairness and meaning are what's most important, how do we experience either from the purely utilitarian act of buying something?

Enter the *buycott*.

Americans have always used the marketplace to express themselves, and boycotts have long been a popular strategy for consumer activism. Though generally accepted as an effective method of protest, the actual outcome of boycotting is complicated and often misunderstood. As widely reported in 2012, the CEO of upscale fast-food chain Chick-fil-A made anti–gay marriage remarks that were met with wide outrage. LGBTQ+ organizations, alongside other socially progressive groups, quickly organized boycotts of Chick-fil-A restaurants, and the news coverage painted a picture of a company headed for disaster. At the same time, however, conservative groups mobilized support for Chick-fil-A through a phenomenon known colloquially as a *buycott*. The buycott, designed to reward the company for taking a public position they supported, more than counteracted the boycott, and Chick-fil-A actually reported record sales (Jeltsen, 2012). Even though most Americans polled supported gay marriage, the failed boycott effort showed they represented a *silent* majority. The buycott actively galvanized supporters, while the opposition existed mainly in principle (Graham, 2019).

Those most affected by boycotts are sometimes not even the intended targets. The boycotts of British Petroleum (BP) after the Deepwater Horizon oil spill in 2010 hurt unrelated and independent gas station owners much more than the oil company itself (Carlock, 2010). At that time, BP owned less than 5 percent of its more than eleven thousand branded stations in the United States, and the biggest pain for station owners came from lost sales from higher-margin convenience store items like chips and pop (in Michigan, we say *pop*, instead of *soda*). Similarly, single-day gas boycotts, though popular, have close-to-zero effect on gas prices and the financial health of oil companies. These protests merely create longer lines at filling stations the next day or encourage consumers to top off their tanks the day before. It's not abstinence. It's just rearrangement of purchasing habits, and it perfectly illustrates a major problem with boycotts: people often don't understand or stick to them. It isn't that boycotts are completely ineffective; rather, their effect on a business is usually more *reputational* than economic. It's a moral reckoning, not a monetary one, and highly publicized boycotts are most likely to change a company's *behavior*, not sales.

In our industry, achieving meaning through abstaining appears elusive as well. The acquisition of Chicago's own Goose Island Beer Company by Anheuser-Busch InBev in 2011 sent waves through the world of craft beer. Goose Island has long been a beacon of innovation in brewing, and many of its supporters throughout the country were appalled by its sale to the "Evil Empire." I watched with interest as local merchants announced boycotts, and beer enthusiasts abided by them. But over the next few years, the calls for abstinence grew fainter. Largely because of the quality of its coveted Bourbon County series, Goose Island products slowly began to reappear in craft circles. The prevailing reasoning was that by continuing to drink Goose Island, craft consumers could actively participate in shaping the company for the better. Uninterrupted consumption might convince the new ownership to keep the beer and the people employed there the same, whereas maintaining a boycott might only encourage the corporate overlords to change the culture and cut corners in the way many feared they would. Plus, *the beer was good.* That alone was almost enough. It was a war AB InBev won by both attrition and attention to quality, and even the staunchest of opponents eventually gave in or stopped caring. Consumption usually wins. We must understand that.

To wit, *buycotts* have become an increasingly powerful tool and reflect a marketplace behavior we can expect to see more and more often. A 2018 study by PR firm Weber Shandwick showed that in the last two years, buycotters took an average of 5.7 supportive actions versus 4.5 from boycotters (Weber Shandwick, Inc., 2018). And buycotts are only expected to grow in number. It's clear that we increasingly define ourselves by what we do, not by what we don't.

BE CONSPICUOUS

This new world of buycotts and social media justice can strike fear in the heart of the small business owner. And we haven't always steered clear of controversy. Some of our famous guests have deeply polarized our customer base; visits from Oprah and former first daughter Chelsea Clinton in particular brought about angry reactions and calls to boycott. But they never amounted to anything. When confronted about either incident, Max and I spoke honestly about the reasons we hosted these guests: We're *small business owners*. We disarmed most of the anger by emphasizing just that. We weren't making a political statement. We're just hardworking guys with families and small children who were afforded visits by famous people. Ideology aside, shouldn't we all root for that? Except for one bar deciding not to carry our beer anymore (which later reversed that), neither incident actually hurt us. In both cases, we were back to slinging beers and pizza as we always had the next day. Our longstanding reputation for ethical community work derailed any half-formed attempt to allow any one controversial incident to define us.

Ultimately, giving is the perfect antidote to living in fear. Instead of trying to avoid trouble, we should be active in defining our companies positively. Whether it's giving in the community or treating staff members fairly, it's always most important to consider the needs of the people we depend on *first*. The key to combating mistakes we make along the way is authenticity. Apologies have to be real. *Mea culpa* is no substitute for *mea maxima culpa*. But unlike our larger competitors, we can actually benefit from the mistakes we make. Indeed, more than a few of our long-term customer relationships began with a complaint, and going above and beyond to fix problems allowed us to earn trust and forge a bond that we might not have otherwise.

There's a little bit of rebellion in every glass of micro-brewed beer we drink, every plastic straw we refuse, and every bit of fairness we demonstrate. Each is a rebuke to the big, intractable corporations that are unable to adjust to the changing needs of the people they serve. In the final analysis, that's why small business is so special. We possess both the vantage point to see problems as they occur and the flexibility and authority to actually fix them. But as we've learned, this type of benefit isn't limited to customers. As Rachel's unfortunate experience taught us, transparency has advantages that permeate nearly every aspect of the small business.

CHAPTER 10

WIN-WINS ARE EVERYWHERE

·····················

"COMPETING AT THE HIGHEST LEVEL IS NOT ABOUT
WINNING. IT'S ABOUT PREPARATION, COURAGE,
UNDERSTANDING AND NURTURING YOUR PEOPLE,
AND HEART. WINNING IS THE RESULT."

— JOE TORRE

JEAN SILBAR IS A tireless, passionate advocate for her work. And confident, too. "We're going to pack your place," she told us back in June 2014. "You won't know what hit you."

We laughed. She didn't. On event night, supporters of her nonprofit, Comprehensive Therapy Center, arrived in force. Our kitchen was overwhelmed with food orders from dinner until close, and though I did my best to help, it wasn't nearly enough. We were staffed for a regular Monday, and this dinner rush felt more like a Saturday. Jean and her development director Summer, by contrast, were the picture of calm as they welcomed customers and directed traffic as if they owned the place. They split duties; Jean spoke to each table, while Summer ran take-out pizzas to customers in the parking lot in order to drive up food sales without sacrificing precious table space. They were sharply focused on making the most out of their fundraising opportunity, and it was inspiring to watch.

The surge proved too much for our team, however. The back-of-house staff was exhausted, and many customers were unable to be seated due to long ticket times and left upset. Although I was embarrassed, I was in awe of how hard CTC worked and how much its members embraced the opportunity we gave them. Plus, the financial upside was obvious. The day's sales were the biggest we had ever seen on a Monday. We had been hosting these fundraising events for more than a year, and though they were generally busier than normal Mondays, we never had one like this. If we could find a way to repeat this success by showing our other nonprofit partners how CTC did it, Mondays were about to change forever. After the dust settled, I knew I had serious problems to confront, although, as people often say and I grew to hate hearing, they were *good problems*.

....

Win-wins rarely begin that way. Our approach to Monday benefit nights certainly must have seemed lopsided from the outside. After all, we were working twice as hard for half the money. But we were betting the pain was temporary and hoped that the benefits (whenever they finally arrived) would define us for the life of our business. And that's exactly what happened. We've outpaced growth trends in an already fast-growing industry, attracted talented employees and retained them at a rate far better than the national average, and built a quality brand that is recognized throughout Michigan. We did all of this while being a key partner in the growth and vitality of our neighborhood. But it wasn't just about what we *did*. I'm positive that our success had just as much to do with what we *learned* from our nonprofit partners such as Jean.

While I had known her for years, I didn't realize until that night just how good she is at what she does. Her organization offers a wide range of free programming for physically and developmentally disabled children and adults with a wide range of diagnoses, but what she really does is bring out the best in everyone she meets. Jean and Summer showed us how to be a stronger company by bringing our established system to a crashing halt, sort of like Schumpeter's *creative destruction*, but, you know . . . with pizza. They forced us to brainstorm different ways to prepare for events, and as our execution improved, the memories of empty tables on Mondays began to fade. CTC demonstrated the true potential of bringing our nonprofit partners *into* our business. Thanks to them, we finally experienced the type of mutual benefit we had envisioned from the beginning.

TWO MITTENS IPA: FROM LOSE-LOSE TO WIN-WIN

Borrowing from the lexicon of game theory mathematics, the art of negotiation suggests every negotiation results in one of three outcomes: *Lose-Lose* (where neither party achieves a desirable result), *Win-Lose* (where one party achieves a positive result and one doesn't), and *Win-Win* (where both parties achieve a mutually beneficial end). Win-wins are also known as *non-zero-sum* outcomes and are obviously the most desirable. That's what we aim for with every partnership. Unlike fiercely competitive corporations, small businesses dispel the notion daily that someone has to lose for us to benefit. We share customers and ideas and, to some extent, common goals. To this end, companies like ours are more reflective of an evolving world.

Author and journalist Robert Wright, in his book *Nonzero*, theorized that as complexity increases in our world, so does the likelihood of achieving non-zero-sum outcomes. A prime example is the way in which electronic communication has made it easier for people around the globe to share new goods and ideas. Wright contends that cooperation has the potential to provide far greater rewards than direct competition does, and this has certainly been our experience; the bigger our network and experience grew, the more we were able to connect ideas and people to achieve the most benefit for all. But it wasn't just about objective complexity; increased *connection* is the true key to driving us forward, and it's what sets us apart from large corporations. Small businesses build long-term relationships by creating meaningful bonds in a way that big companies can't.

When we broaden our goals beyond merely maximizing profitability, a sea of unique opportunities appears. We found one of them in white-knuckle fashion when, thanks to the help of some dedicated friends, we were able to turn a major brew-house error into a life-changing gift. It was perhaps our biggest Win-Win to date because it arose from a total Lose-Lose situation.

LOSE-LOSE

Our brewery's staple beer is Country Strong IPA. In the world of craft beer, where there are nearly as many variations of styles as there are enthusiasts, the IPA still reigns supreme. Country Strong has been our best-selling beer since it first went on tap in early 2013. It has so many dedicated drinkers, in fact, that when there is some batch-to-batch inconsistency (not uncommon in a small brew house), the more astute customers notice and relish in point-ing it out.

One night in the winter of 2017, a customer sent his pint back, claiming it didn't taste like Country Strong. I overheard the complaint and went behind the bar to pour myself a sample, positive he was mistaken or had been served the wrong beer. But sure enough, he was right. The taste was definitely different but not nearly as much as the *color*. Country Strong pours a golden yellow, and the beer I held in my hands was nearly red.

How did this happen? The brewers retraced their steps all the way back to the brew day and surmised that a bag of dark malt had likely been mis-marked by the supplier (which happens occasionally) and added to the grain we mashed, producing a redder, maltier version of Country Strong. It wasn't a bad beer, by any stretch of the imagination; in fact, it was quite good. But the differences were enough to be noticed, and our first concern was damage to the brand. This was our flagship, and we had very recently made a major investment to put it into statewide distribution in 12-ounce cans.

As brewery owners, this is one of the toughest decisions Max and I ever have to make: dump a questionable beer (and with it, many thousands of dollars) down the drain, or serve it and risk doing long-term damage to our reputation?

LOSE: Damage to our reputation
LOSE: Dumping valuable beer

As we mulled this painful decision, we kept coming back to the idea that the beer was still good; it just wasn't Country Strong. Selling it under a different, re-branded name started to seem like a viable third option.

THE MITTEN STATE

Years before we ever brewed a beer together, we had been a little scared of the Mitten State apparel company. When Max and I trademarked our business name, we researched every other Michigan business with "Mitten" in its name and, of course, came across the Mitten State. Fortunately, we were the only company trying to use "Mitten" in craft beer, and our trademark was issued, but we were still nervous. The Mitten State had built a strong business and brand—its bumper stickers and T-shirts were everywhere—and we weren't sure how the company would feel about another startup with the same eponymous distinction. So instead of just crossing our fingers and hoping for the best, we decided to visit the company's shop and address the issue head-on. Will and Mike, the owners and the only employees at the time, looked at each other with trepidation when we introduced ourselves, but, thankfully, the discussion quickly turned into ways we could work together and ended with them agreeing to design our brewery apparel. A partnership and a friendship were born.

In 2015, the Mitten Brewing Company brewed a beer called "Two Mittens Red IPA," in collaboration with the Mitten State apparel company, the purpose of which was to promote our brands. People often assumed we were related companies anyway, and we didn't really mind. We were both proud of each other and saw some benefit to just leaning into it. The beer sold well, but we considered it a one-off and had no plans to make it again. That is, until this reddish batch of Country Strong two years later. It had so many of the same attributes as our previous collaboration beer, Two Mittens Red IPA, that we were confident we could brand and sell it that way. We invited the Mitten State owners to the pub to discuss ways to use this turn of events to our mutual advantage.

We learned that Will and his new partner Scott (Mike had tragically died in an auto accident several years earlier) were looking for ways to make a bigger difference in their community, having opened up a retail shop in our neighborhood a year prior. They had done some work with national charities in the past but were interested in getting involved with what the Mitten Foundation was doing on a local level. This was music to our ears. We had wanted to engage more area businesses in our mission, and Will and Scott were a perfect fit: their company, the Mitten State, was a successful and growing Michigan-centric brand, their media reach was huge, and because of our similar names, the public already associated us together, to some extent.

Max and I agreed to make this accidental version of Two Mittens beer a foundation project and brainstormed with Will and Scott over a few (many) pints about what type of benefit made the most sense. The question we kept asking ourselves was: "What can two Mittens do?" The obvious answer was that actual mittens keep people warm. We laughed about it, but this silly premise was how we stumbled upon the idea to bring warmth to our disadvantaged neighbors during the cold Michigan winters. We were excited about our renewed partnership, and both Mitten companies agreed to put skin in the game. Max and I offered to donate a dollar from every pint of Two Mittens beer sold, and Will and Scott agreed to design a T-shirt and donate $10 from each sale.

The only thing we were missing was . . . well, the actual idea. Not an ideal way to start a project. We talked about using the money to buy warm clothes for those who couldn't afford them, but we all agreed it felt too rote and was probably only marginally useful. There had to be something more meaningful out there. I knew from experience that we likely weren't the best judges of what that might be, so I set up a meeting with our neighborhood organization.

Its members agreed our idea wouldn't accomplish much. Area shelters were largely addressing that problem already, so they pointed us in a different direction: Their office received calls on almost a daily basis from neighbors afraid their heat would be shut off, due to nonpayment. This was a common problem, one that worsened each winter, due to rising energy costs and decreases in the federal funding of LIHEAP (Low-Income Home Energy Assistance Program). Though funding for the federal program had been at an all-time high after the 2008 housing collapse, its appropriation had decreased every year since as the crisis faded into the past (LIHEAP, 2018). The problem was still very real in our neighborhood, however, and more and more people who depended on the stipend were finding themselves ineligible. Right away, we saw this was a better way to put ourselves between our neighbors and the cold. We decided to wrap them in the Two Mittens program and pay their past-due bills until the money ran out.

FROM LOSE-LOSE TO WIN-LOSE

Our neighborhood organization had the most direct route to our neighbors in need, and its members agreed not only to draft and distribute the Energy Assistance Grant applications, but also to vet the applicants to ensure the grants went to the people with the greatest need. People working on the Two Mittens project focused on getting the word out. We announced the program on local news stations and our social media platforms where it was shared and re-shared hundreds of times. Public enthusiasm for the idea was so high that we were afraid we'd have far more applications than we could ever accommodate. But two weeks before the deadline, we had a curious problem. We had received only one application.

WIN: The reputations of both Mitten companies
LOSE: Unreached applicants

We were mystified. Considering the sheer number of people who were sharing the information, not to mention the neighbors who called and asked for help outright, we couldn't understand why the apps hadn't poured in. The support from our customers was obviously there because we watched both the beer and the shirts sell quickly. But there we were, with thousands of dollars and no one to take the money. We wondered whether perhaps the application was too long or difficult to understand? Was it because we had a mild winter, and people didn't need as much help? Was it because, even though we had Spanish-language applications available, non–English speakers didn't know where to find them? Perhaps it was similar to the struggles the federal government encounters with SNAP (a.k.a. food stamps). Many people either aren't aware of the benefits or wrongly assume they don't qualify. Whatever the reason, it was obvious we weren't reaching the people who needed assistance, and we were running out of time; the application deadline and warmer weather were approaching fast.

We kept trying things, hoping the solution would present itself. We hung up fliers inside area stores and nearby nonprofits. We shared the information with as many people as possible, but after two more weeks of work, we still had only one application. We planned to volunteer at a Feeding America food pantry the day before the February 28th deadline, so, as a last-ditch effort, we brought a stack of twenty applications along with us. As we handed out pizza slices to the people waiting in the cold, we began talking to them about the grant. Within a few minutes, all the applications were gone, and the people in line were filling them out frantically.

It was so unbelievably obvious that we missed it entirely. *These were the people who needed this program.* They had been right in front of us, week after week. Television and the Internet weren't the way to reach them; we had to meet them in person, and the obvious intersection between food insecurity and heat insecurity was where to find them. We realized the paternalism that had plagued this idea since the beginning was still with us. We were once again reminded that personal connection is the key to understanding need. *We have to meet people where they are, not where we think they should be.* We can't assume that the virtue of an idea alone will carry it forth because time and time again, our own experiences show us it won't.

FROM WIN-LOSE TO WIN-WIN

We finally had enough applications, and Dana, armed with a stack of past-due bills and our foundation bank card, spent an afternoon on the phone with the gas company. It's hard to describe the happiness I felt as I watched her make the stress and shame of these past-due bills disappear.

WIN: The reputations of both Mitten companies
WIN: Every single applicant

The people who benefited came from all different walks of life. They included single parents with young children, seniors suffering from physical disabilities, and, most heartbreakingly, two victims of domestic abuse. One applicant had fled her abusive husband with her children but was unable to activate the utilities in their new apartment until her past-due bills were settled. Our involvement helped her start a new, safer life for her children. The other applicant was a Hispanic woman (Dana did her best on the phone, but by her own admission, most of her Spanish is gleaned from *Dora the Explorer*) who, along with her four children, had also recently left an abusive husband and was in a similar predicament: trying to start over but hampered by past debts. Dana wept as she spoke with each applicant and heard the relief and joy in their voices. The process changed us forever.

The Two Mittens project taught us a lot about the many reasons why people move in and out of crises of poverty. Investing this time and energy with our neighbors permanently improved our understanding of their struggles and showed us that even the direst situations can be redeemed. After all, the money we raised almost never existed. Not only was the very idea borne from a huge and potentially costly mistake, but we made another along the way that almost killed it. Ultimately, we learned that much like the way organizations such as Feeding America provide value by preventing excess food from being squandered, we, too, were capable of turning waste into transformative action. What a shame it would have been to dump 620 gallons of beer and never learn this lesson.

TWO MITTENS, 2.0

We were very aware of just how much the Two Mittens project had benefited from us troubleshooting our mistakes, and its third undertaking began with this in mind. We all agreed that besides the obvious struggles we encountered in finding applicants, the Two Mittens program could be improved in other ways. There's a fair argument to be made that it was little more than a stopgap for some of the people it benefited. What resonated most with the board was the obvious relationship between domestic abuse and poverty, and as winter approached the following year, we started with an intentional focus on survivors of domestic abuse. We decided to go right to the experts.

Safe Haven Ministries, one of our previous nonprofit partners, is one of the largest area emergency shelters for survivors of abuse. On top of providing no-cost and confidential shelter space, Safe Haven offers many non-residential services, including case management, support groups, and trauma intervention for children. The organization works around the clock to stop the cycle of abuse by providing survivors with the time, safety, and education to build a future for themselves. And it works. Most who pass through Safe Haven do not return to the abusive environments that brought them there. Partnering with the organization directly ensured that our gift would provide relief in the truest sense; the crises confronted by the people they serve are seldom (though not seldom enough), immediate, and temporary. People leave Safe Haven well on their way toward rehabilitation.

Safe Haven's slogan is "Love Shouldn't Hurt," and in light of the new partnership, the Two Mittens project was reborn as "Love." The Mitten State donated from its Michigan Love apparel series, and we rebranded our Two Mittens beer as "Love IPA." The renewed approach resonated strongly with our customers and even our business neighbors. DeVries Jewelers, our good friends who have mercifully helped Max and me with many an eleventh-hour anniversary gift for our lovely wives, asked to jump onto our effort and offered to match $3,000 of our contributions. We were overwhelmed by their generosity, although it was admittedly challenging to find a way to work a jewelry store into all of our Mitten-centric marketing. But much like the ones that Jean and Summer had created for us back in 2014, this was a *good problem.*

CHAPTER 11

WHAT SUSTAINS US?

....

> "A LIFE IS NOT IMPORTANT EXCEPT
> IN THE IMPACT IT HAS ON OTHER LIVES."
> — JACKIE ROBINSON

"JACK REALLY ENJOYED HIS time at the Mitten," Ron began his message to Max and me. Ron was Ron Wade, the longtime marketing director of the Detroit Tigers. Jack was Hall of Fame pitcher Jack Morris.

"I was escorting Jack around the ballpark on Saturday, and he raved about his time there," Ron continued.

We were enormously proud. Jack wasn't exactly Oprah, but he had certainly played a bigger role in our childhood. Max and I always dreamed the Mitten might someday be a place where our boyhood heroes would gravitate. With visits from the Tigers' Winter Caravan the previous year and now this event with Jack Morris, it looked like that dream might actually become a reality.

Anchored by a keynote address from Jack, the luncheon we'd hosted a day earlier capped off two months of fundraising to provide school uniforms for our neighborhood elementary school, Harrison Park. This project was our first as a foundation, and though we didn't know it, it was also the first step on our path toward sustainability. Like all of our most worthwhile undertakings, it began as something entirely different from what it became.

More than two months prior, we received a letter from Stephen, the school's social worker, asking for help in buying new or gently used uniforms. Many parents struggled with purchasing the clothes required by the school district, and our neighborhood organization referred Stephen to us as a potential partner. The school maintained a small stock of secondhand uniforms in Stephen's office, but he often handed them out with no system in place to replenish them. Though it might seem like a superficial problem, he explained that a lack of access to school uniforms presents a number of disciplinary problems, including chronic absenteeism. We jumped at the chance to help. The need was hyperlocal and timely, and although we had donated to a scholarship fund for college-bound students there in 2014, we had never done any work directly inside the school. Plus, we had received our nonprofit status only weeks prior and felt it would be an excellent first project.

Our benefit night netted $2,500, shy of our $3,000 target, and the shortfall bothered us. Although the goal was arbitrary, and we were under no actual obligation to keep raising more money, we were hungry to surpass our goal on this first project. We needed to get creative.

A PERFECT PITCH

We learned the West Michigan Whitecaps were hosting an evening autograph event with Jack Morris at the ballpark, and we had an idea. Could we convince him to make a lunch appearance at the Mitten the same day? We asked the Whitecaps' front office for help, and its staff went to bat (*pun intended*) for us. Jack agreed to help for just a small fraction of his normal fee. We did the math and figured we could sell enough tickets to make the lunch run at least $500 in the black, so we scheduled it and started to promote it to our mug clubbers.

The response started slow but gained steam, and by the morning of the event, we'd sold the last handful of tickets. Dana and I spent the morning carefully appointing the upstairs taproom, but when we surveyed it, I felt a little self-conscious. I worried Jack would balk (*Last one. Sorry. I've been waiting this entire book to make baseball puns.*) when he walked in and saw the scratched maple floors, crooked windows, and wobbly, hand-built tables. I mean, this was a guy whose baseball cards I'd collected (and still have in my basement in protective sleeves). But Dana reminded me why people come here in the first place: it's *because* of those things. And for celebrity guests, we've found the Mitten is a welcome change from the stuffy banquets and formal affairs they're usually invited to. We learned that lesson in expensive fashion during the Tigers' visit the previous winter. We had hired an outside chef to prepare baked salmon and gourmet sides for the players, but it turned out they just wanted to drink beer and eat pizza. It was their last of many stops that weekend, and the road-weary team was excited to be somewhere the players could finally relax. We ended up with sixty portions of untouched salmon, but the staff sure ate like royalty.

The room was already buzzing with mug clubbers when Jack arrived. He had a famously brusque reputation with the sporting press, which many believe kept him out of the Hall of Fame until the Veterans Committee voted him in, in 2017, but he was engaging and personable with our guests. I relished the opportunity to introduce him as "five-time All-Star, four-time

World Series champion, World Series MVP, the winningest pitcher of the 1980s and the only one Sparky Anderson didn't dare to pull!"

Jack smiled at the warm welcome. We hadn't given him any parameters for his remarks—just that he talk a little about his playing days—but, thankfully, he went above and beyond and brought the real value to our event. He captivated the group of die-hard Tigers fans with candid stories from the 1984 season and the legendary 35 and 5 start that propelled them to a World Series victory. He further indulged us by taking photos with attendees in our reclaimed Tiger Stadium seats. As I watched our guests relive their sunny memories of the greatest Detroit team ever to take the field, I forgot all about our wobbly tables and scuffed floors and felt stupid for worrying about them in the first place.

STOPGAP

The lunch put us well over the top of our $3,000 goal. We took a moment to soak the whole thing in but quickly turned our attention back to uniforms. We had enough cash to buy 300, but Stephen advised us to make an initial purchase of 100 and earmark the rest of the money for future uniform purchases. He wasn't sure how many the school actually needed at a time, but we were all fairly confident that 100 would be plenty.

It turns out that was only enough for six months.

The school families took full advantage of the gift and showed us the need was far greater than we thought. It wasn't just about putting uniforms in a closet; it was about reducing the stigma of poverty, improving attendance, and cutting down on disciplinary actions. And it did all those things. We were happy with the results but wondered about the long-term solution. Would we have to keep raising thousands for this cause each year? I doubted our ability to maintain that kind of momentum for a project that was supposed to be a one-time intervention. Time passed, and in the spring of the following year, we purchased another hundred uniforms at Stephen's request, but he, too, was of a mind that there had to be a better way to solve this problem, other than throwing money after it. It felt wasteful. After all, by buying hundreds of new uniforms each year, weren't we just affirming the notion that they were disposable? Was pumping more clothes into circulation actually going to solve this problem, or was it just another example of one-way giving?

THE GIFT THAT KEEPS ON GIVING

Any parent knows that children routinely outgrow uniforms between grade levels. The uniform is then passed down to the next of kin, or it's discarded or given away. Though studies suggest uniforms provide many scholastic benefits, they unfortunately don't have much crossover use outside of school. As a former student who wore a uniform to school, I can say with confidence that wearing a school uniform socially is *not an option*. I couldn't wait to get that thing off when I got home. We brainstormed ways to keep more uniforms in circulation and started circling the idea of a uniform *buyback*. We still had $1,000 earmarked for uniforms; if we could purchase gently used ones from school families for a dollar or two, instead of buying new, we figured our money would go much further. It might even reduce the cost to something the school could manage with only minimal underwriting in the future. A buyback also could be a good way to get school families more invested in the process. Stephen brought our idea to the principal, but it turned out the project had already outgrown us.

The school had been approached by a leadership class at nearby Grand Valley State University, whose focus was to make college an attainable goal for all Harrison Park students. Stephen made them aware of the ongoing uniform issue and its effect on attendance, and the leadership class members designed a uniform swap as their class project. They allowed parents to trade in gently used uniforms for brand-new ones, and they used the ones we had recently donated as part of the "bank" to get started. We attended the program launch, and its efficacy was immediately apparent as more than fifty uniforms were traded in on the first day. Old uniforms were given new life, and the benefit of each dollar we had spent more than doubled.

Our effort may have created the spark, but GVSU fanned it into a flame. The university's involvement ensured the program would only continue to grow and improve as new students enrolled in the curriculum each year. We had no problem moving into a secondary role. Grand Valley's solution was far more efficient than ours, and we were glad to step aside in favor of a better outcome. We recognize that our role as a community leader is sometimes merely to get the ball rolling and demonstrate an interest in helping.

When others notice and decide to get involved, good things usually happen. We see this time and time again. Nine days after we paid off the lunch debt at Suttons Bay schools, we did the same at Fennville Public Schools, a district near our Saugatuck location. The news media once again began to report about it, but the coverage was soon overshadowed by another story: inspired by our Suttons Bay gift, Fetch Brewing Company in nearby Whitehall had cleared the lunch debt from not one but two of its neighboring school districts, donating more than $5,500. The headlines changed to "*another* Michigan brewery clears lunch debts" (Lofton, 2019).

The story traveled wide, diminished not a bit by the amount of coverage we had received the previous week.

A few months later, Little River Casino and Resort in Northern Michigan announced that through a joint effort with twenty-five neighboring businesses, they raised more than $14,000 and cleared all the lunch debt for students in their home of Manistee County. They, too, had been inspired by our gesture. "The Mitten Brewing Company ['s gifts] got me thinking a lot about what we can do together," said the casino's food and beverage director (Grabowski, 2019). Several weeks after that, forty-two Applebees restaurants throughout Michigan held lunch debt fundraisers for the communities they do business in, and Trail Point Brewing cleared lunch debts in its home of Allendale. As each story appeared in the news, we were thrilled and felt a little like proud parents—albeit a little self-conscious. It was such a cheap and easy way to do some good; it felt like we were getting far more praise than we deserved.

But sometimes things really are that easy, despite our best efforts to complicate them. Making school better for kids with barriers is an incredible opportunity with a low price tag. Our modest gift—which more than paid for itself—sparked a movement that has eliminated the lunch debt of thousands of Michigan students so far. And I have a feeling there are more gifts to come.

LOOKING TO THE FUTURE

Sustainable solutions like the uniform swap are the next frontier for the Mitten Foundation. *Sustainability* is a broad term but is usually used to define self-perpetuating growth that endures without the depletion or exploitation of finite resources. It's critical to understand, however, that sustainability is more of a process than a destination.

There's also an important distinction between *sustaining* something and *sustainability*. To sustain an action is to strengthen and support it, and the act of sustaining something makes it better, stronger, and more likely to thrive on its own. In other words, only by *sustaining* something in the first place can we ever encourage its *sustainability*. When Max and I broke ground on our block, we took a risk that later encouraged more investment as a result. Now every new business that appears in our neighborhood gives strength to the rest, and our community as a whole becomes more sustainable by virtue of our collective success. Better to be a district than a destination, we always say. The more thriving businesses that surround us, the more patronage we are all able to attract.

Giving is an important part of sustaining a neighborhood, but it's not always about practical needs. An important part of improving lives is supporting things that better our outlook on life itself. Enrichment opportunities create happier and healthier individuals who are more likely to escape from cycles of disadvantage and help others do the same. I've seen this value firsthand, and it's why I have difficulty accepting binary conclusions about who we should help and who we should not. A rising tide raises all ships, and there's no telling what effect an investment in a person will truly have on his or her future. As we learned with the heating assistance grants, even the smallest gesture can make a big difference in someone's life. *And we have to keep trying different things.* Though it's tempting to search for a single obvious solution to problems, it's usually a combination of many small fixes with varying degrees of effectiveness that ends up making the difference.

We helped send twenty-five teenagers from our neighboring high school to Washington, D.C., through Close Up, a nonprofit governmental immersion program that "seeks to inform, inspire, and empower young people to exercise the rights and accept the responsibilities of citizens in a democracy." We saw the value in encouraging students to increase their role in the political process. There are no doubt more desperate and timely causes, but these students could very well alter the course of our world someday. We consider investing in positive outcomes for their future to be money well spent.

We must also recognize how culture enriches our lives. While it may have been at odds with our giving mission, we've sponsored ballet performances, horseback riding, and live music festivals. In 2018, we turned our Grand Rapids taproom into a free gallery for disabled artists during ArtPrize, the world's largest art competition. Our partners in this pursuit showed us the value of inspiring expression and fighting disability stigma, and many of the pieces we displayed ended up being sold. Help aspiring artists jump-start their path toward becoming working professionals? I'm in.

Sustainability isn't just a question of whether an action depletes resources; there is a wide spectrum of success that almost always begins with an investment in *people*. That's our role to play. My favorite thing is to see work we've started grow beyond our doors and take on a life of its own.

INSPECT WHAT YOU EXPECT

In the winter of 2018, I felt as if some of our nonprofit work wasn't connecting with our staff. It was a familiar feeling. We had been working with many of the same assumptions for the last four years, and the staff had grown and changed a lot since then. Though I regularly checked in with everyone conversationally, I was afraid that approach might have stifled critical input, and it had. I took a survey, and it revealed that while our team was still most passionate about local causes, a growing number of its members, especially among the younger staff, were interested in supporting national and even international causes—specifically, disaster relief. This was new. I was surprised and wanted to dig deeper when Jeff, one of our most recent brew-house hires, brought us the perfect way to test it.

For several months prior, wildfire had ravaged Butte County in northern California. The "Camp Fire," as it came to be known, was the deadliest and most destructive fire in the state's history, killing scores of people and destroying nearly twenty thousand buildings. In nearby Chico, the Sierra Nevada Brewing Co. decided to brew a beer to raise funds for the victims and challenged other breweries throughout the country to join them. They established the Camp Fire Relief Fund and shared the recipe for Resilience Butte County Proud IPA with breweries that elected to participate. Jeff, who had come to our company for the chance to do things like this, had been following the story closely and asked whether we could take part. The staff survey results were fresh in my mind, and I said yes.

We were the first brewery in Michigan to sign up and the nineteenth overall. Ultimately, more than twelve hundred breweries answered the call, and vendors from all over the country organized to donate the raw materials (Snider, 2018). When we announced our participation, the staff members came to life in a way we hadn't seen in months. Resilience IPA went on tap a few weeks later, and they made it our top-selling beer. I had no idea they could be this passionate about something happening more than two thousand miles away, but we saw right away how mistakenly operating under the same assumptions for the last four years had likely handicapped our giving efforts.

The board voted to allow the staff to choose *at least* one nonprofit each year. Employees were always involved to some degree, but we had never given them complete free rein. It was time to make it formal and intentional. Besides disaster relief, their survey results also indicated a clear preference for wildlife rehabilitation, and in August 2019 they selected a nonprofit called All Species Kinship. A.S.K. was fostering a pit bull rescued from a dog-fighting ring. He had been used as a "bait dog" and suffered numerous injuries and infections before being saved by the police. A.S.K. was seeking funds for medical care, and the staff members jumped all over it. They dubbed the poor nameless pooch "Al Canine," and the event night ended up being our biggest ever, passing the previous record set by Jean and CTC. These two partnerships—borne 100 percent from the staff's affinities and not the board's—were humbling reminders of our limitations. Opening up the process is sometimes the best way to keep good efforts going.

THE GRADUAL GROUNDSWELL

Our most worthwhile efforts started small and improved over time, and that's probably the best way to go about it. When it comes to giving, easy success is often its undoing. See the 2014 Amyotrophic Lateral Sclerosis (ALS) Ice Bucket Challenge. The campaign, which challenged people to dump a bucket of ice water on their heads, was designed to raise awareness and funds for ALS research. Participants posted videos on their social media networks and challenged their followers to do the same. It was one of the most successful nonprofit campaigns ever and raised more than $115 million for the national ALS Association. But the following year, the same approach raised less than 1 percent of the previous year's total. The campaign had flatlined.

Scientific American observed that viral social campaigns rarely maintain their momentum once they pass their original tipping point (van der Linden, 2017). It's easy to see why they take off: they're designed to push specific emotional and psychological levers that compel people to act. But this is also their downfall; viral campaigns are often defined by an *extrinsic* desire to do something good. Extrinsic motivations are well-intentioned but unessential, shallow, and unlikely to be sustained. A sense of competition or challenge may be helpful in spreading awareness among peers, but it doesn't create a deep and ongoing connection with a cause. *Intrinsic*, or unconditional, motivation has been shown to encourage helping behavior over time. *Scientific American* concluded that "in order to make viral altruism stick, more gradual and deeper engagement with a social cause is required over a sustained period of time."

This is obvious when we step back and take away all the terminology and the technology. We all understand that the more we actually care about something, the more likely we are to get involved and stay involved. The more we care, the harder we work. The harder we work, the more we improve.

In 2014, when the Mitten Brewing Company decided to collaborate with our friends Will and Mike, the owners of the apparel company the Mitten State, we did it for self-promotion and to celebrate all things Michigan. We called the joint effort of our two companies "Two Mittens." Yet we didn't fully develop the charitable aspect of Two Mittens until 2017, when our two companies began struggling to find a way to bring warmth to our neighbors. In the same vein, the partnership that formed Love Shouldn't Hurt consisted of three businesses with a plan to raise $10,000 for a domestic abuse shelter. The third effort was the most organized and influential to date, bonding twenty area craft beverage producers in a shared show of support for the shelter. Each new step was built on the previous one's success. When we work with the right people on the right things, we get better. It's that simple.

Ultimately, giving isn't that different from entrepreneurship. Small businesses depend on the same type of organic growth for sustained success, and changing demographics are on their side. Citing positive cash flow and increases in hiring and investment, a 2018 Wells Fargo and Gallup survey showed that optimism among American small businesses is at its highest point since the survey began fifteen years prior (Wells Fargo Works, 2018). And these benefits aren't just enjoyed by businesses. Certainly, our block here in Grand Rapids has been improved by the small companies that inhabit it. Property values increase, new opportunities for employment arise, and the surrounding schools and nonprofits are strengthened.

But it isn't easy.

One has to be suited for it, and we are. Small businesses are the result of hard work, faith, and dedication to a higher purpose. We are brick and mortar, blood and sweat, muscle and sinew. We form deep relationships with our customers, teams, and neighbors. We depend on innovation to survive. We are sewn into the fabric of America, dotting the entire landscape, and can touch every corner of it in unique ways. We can go deeper than any single company or campaign ever could. Every strong commitment, whether we begin it or successfully complete it, lends strength and greater participation to the next. It's what makes us the great hope for giving. We can reach people that the great nonprofits and NGOs of our world, which do unimaginably difficult and important work daily, simply cannot—all because of what we do best. Whether it's school kids with dirty uniforms or lunch with Hall of Fame pitchers, it's our job to always do the type of work that makes our world a better place in the best way we know how.

CHAPTER 12

A CALL TO ACTION

....

> "YESTERDAY'S HOME RUNS DON'T WIN TOMORROW'S GAMES."
> — BABE RUTH

SEVEN YEARS INTO MY career as both a brewery owner and an aspiring philanthropist, I've learned a lot about both disciplines. Embarrassing mistakes, broken relationships, and disappointments are all wreckage alongside the path of our progress. But it is progress. All of it. It's our history, and the mistakes and shortcomings have been the most indispensable parts of shaping it. What matters most is where we end up, not that we got there perfectly.

To me, giving is about decoding the promise within all of us. Sometimes it's buried deep, but it's always there. That's how writing was for me. In *On Writing*, famed author Stephen King compares the process to digging up a fossil; it's about carefully extracting what you have to say over time and allowing the results to reveal themselves. Trying to yank it out of the ground right away can damage it forever. I found that to be very true, whether in composing music or writing this book.

Finding what moves us to give and how to amplify it was the challenge of a lifetime. At times I felt ill prepared for it; I felt self-conscious about my experience and sometimes like an imposter in both fields. After all, I'm not the world's shrewdest businessman—or the best or most cutting-edge philanthropist. Not by a long shot. I'm not a millionaire, nor have I given away millions. The Mitten Foundation's giving totals are pretty modest by many standards and downright laughable compared to those of companies such as Walmart, which gives away hundreds of millions annually. But the Mitten Foundation's gifts certainly made a bigger difference for our neighborhood, and that's what makes them special. Recognizing that isn't hubris. I don't believe what I have to say is revolutionary or even difficult to apply. After all, I'm not suggesting that we all need to be necessarily more generous, although that certainly wouldn't be a poor result. My goal is to create a different understanding of our platform as small business owners and the unique opportunities it affords us.

In my process of "digging up the fossil," I kept coming back to "The Parable of the River." It's easy to see its message at work in our lives. Whether it's our ability to recognize the suffering of our neighbors or the innate desire to be better at everything we do, it encapsulates what is best about us: our undeniable impulse to help those in need. Though the complexity of our lives leads us to think that things are more fractured than they are, I'm inclined to believe—whether you call it destiny, Adam Smith's Invisible Hand, or Robert Wright's conclusion in *Nonzero*—that despite myriad setbacks, humanity does indeed have an overall direction, and it's a good one.

I've read my mother's dog-eared copy of *Walden* many times, and Thoreau's experience has always provided me with philosophical clarity. "Our life is frittered away by detail," he says. "Simplify. Simplify." We have to recognize the simple truth that giving imbues purpose into our lives and makes them better. "The Parable of the River" ends with the promise of a world that solves its own problems. This story rings true because giving has always evolved to meet our needs.

Since America's birth, its government has struggled to satisfy the requirements of the broad land it serves. But nature abhors a vacuum, and as De Tocqueville observed, Americans are quick to seek their own voluntary associations. What arose from burden sharing among colonists evolved into an ongoing concern for the well-being of our fellow New Worlders. Volunteerism and a sense of civic duty developed alongside burgeoning national pride. Increased urbanization exposed and remedied unsafe working conditions wrought by the Industrial Revolution. Sweeping social reforms dominated nineteenth-century antebellum America, and though it culminated in a bloody and bitter war, we decided slavery was not the course of a great nation. The suffering of soldiers was the impetus for the creation of the American Red Cross.

In the late nineteenth century, America's first great fortunes were made. Owing to the inspiration of financier George Peabody, the founder of the banking institution that would become J.P. Morgan and Co., newly minted aristocrats such as Rockefeller and Carnegie embraced philanthropy as the greatest work of their lives. While the world wars and an economic depression created overwhelming crises in the ensuing decades, Americans boldly mobilized relief for countries ravaged by occupation and sacrificed to build institutions to look after the least among us here at home. In the twentieth century, American philanthropy increasingly focused on advancing the causes of civil rights, and as the millennium approached, globalization brought the world's economic problems into our consciousness.

CHANGE YOUR MIND

Yet despite this overarching trajectory, giving has now stalled among the people who care the most, and nothing short of a fundamental reset in the way we think is required to overcome it. Philanthropist Dan Pallotta once said that the same people making the same gifts won't solve our problems, and it hasn't. Charitable giving has been stuck for fifty years. Unlocking the giving potential of America's small businesses is the key to breaking it wide open.

In recognizing our potential, however, we have to be honest about our failures and half measures. Phrases like *triple bottom line* (3BL) and *corporate social responsibility* (CSR) are fashionable but suffer from a lack of definition. They're ill-defined constructs that disconnect us from the very intentional act of giving. Moreover, they haven't accomplished what they set out to. As we can plainly see, our environment and society are more imperiled than ever. The non-financial objectives of 3BL are often pro forma, and, by admission of the man who coined the phrase, "the triple bottom line has failed to bury the single bottom line paradigm" (Elkington, 2018). Too often, large companies don't attack CSR and 3BL objectives with the same fervor as financial ones. They are viewed as "good to have," not "have to have." They are not deemed truly essential to a company's success.

Even the word *philanthropy* can be an obstacle. It conjures the visage of an elderly, obscenely rich person endowing his or her accumulated wealth to a cause: Ford, Buffet, Gates, et al. *Giving* is more appropriate. Anyone can give. It doesn't require people to accumulate any amount of money first. Our staff members, whether they are dishwashers or managers, overwhelmingly contribute a portion of their bi-weekly paycheck to help fund Mitten Foundation projects. They, along with us, are anything but wealthy. They prove that giving goes beyond the domain of the aristocracy, and it isn't just what we do at the end of our lives because we can't take it with us. Giving can be how we create and enjoy our own prosperity, however modest, during our lifetimes.

WHAT'S PAST IS PROLOGUE

As French historian Paul Hazard wrote, "There's not a tradition which escapes challenge, not an idea, however familiar, which is not assailed; not an authority that is allowed to stand. Institutions of every kind are demolished, and negation is the order of the day" (Bishop, 2017). This has never been more evident than it is in America today.

In a 2016 poll, only 9 percent of Americans responded that they had "a great deal of trust" in Congress (Prahalad, 2017). Nationwide, similar declines in confidence are seen in regard to public schools, the national media, banking institutions, and big corporations. Even our centers of faith have been affected; for the first time since such numbers were recorded, fewer than half of American adults now place a great deal of trust in organized religion, even though it was once considered the country's moral backbone.

Author Bill Bishop, in his influential book *The Big Sort*, showed that as time progresses and Americans become wealthier, more educated, and less concerned about basic survival, they tend to form homogeneous clusters. They cease acquiring knowledge from trusted outside sources and instead seek it only from like-minded acquaintances in what Bishop calls "a feedback loop." This has led to a deepening of extreme ideologies and an increasingly polarized electorate. Yet although we have never been more divided politically, this phenomenon has created a paradoxical byproduct: a thriving small business culture. Neighborhoods attract and create companies that reflect their interests. This is good for both business *and* giving; voluntary redistribution of wealth has been shown to increase when we feel comfortable with our neighbors, while areas that are fiercely dichotomous are less generous. Whether this trend is good or bad for humanity overall remains to be seen, but we can certainly maximize giving's potential by advocating for inclusion and equity in our communities.

Americans are increasingly focused on their individual impact on the world, and small businesses are most able to provide opportunities to demonstrate it. Besides the way we uniquely connect with the marketplace, the modern national economy is arguably driven by us: small businesses are where most Americans find themselves employed on any given day, accounting for 66 percent of all net new jobs since the 1970s (SBA Office of Advocacy, 2018). We alone can transform our culture of consumption into a force for good.

UNLIMITED POTENTIAL

Small businesses can succeed where other institutions can't, and although they may be small in size, they are numerous, profitable, and conscientious. To understand the scale of a unified small business–giving effort, consider the following illustration.

Based on figures reported by *Forbes* (2018), if each of the 30.2 million small businesses in the United States annually donated:

$5.26—They could fund the **March of Dimes** and its work to improve the health of mothers and babies throughout the United States.

$7.02—They could fund **Susan G. Komen**, the nation's largest breast cancer organization.

$7.45—They could fund the **National Multiple Sclerosis Society** and its research, advocacy, and services for families affected by the disease.

$7.68—They could fund the **Humane Society of the United States** and provide services for more than 100,000 animals.

$9.27—They could fund the **Wounded Warrior Project** and provide mental, physical, and financial wellness services for thousands of wounded veterans.

$9.50—They could fund **Toys for Tots**, the U.S. Marine Corp's program to collect and distribute holiday toys to children whose families cannot afford them.

$12.15—They could fund the **Make-A-Wish Foundation** and grant a wish for a child diagnosed with a critical illness every thirty-four minutes.

$28.51—They could fund the **American Cancer Society** and its goal of eliminating cancer.

$65.89—They could fund **Habitat for Humanity International** and build affordable housing all over the world.

$67.55—They could fund **Boys and Girls Club of America** and provide after-school programming for 4 million children, nationwide.

$69.21—They could fund **St. Jude Children's Research Hospital** and provide world-leading disease research and treatment for 8,500 children.

$72.85—They could fund the **Task Force for Global Health** and lead the fight against the most commonly neglected tropical diseases and pandemics in 157 countries around the world.

$90.06—They could fund **Feeding America** and provide food-insecure Americans with 4 billion meals annually, while preventing 3.3 billion pounds of food from going to waste.

$101.32—They could fund the **American Red Cross** and provide emergency assistance and disaster relief throughout the United States.

$129.80—They could fund **United Way of America** and provide vital health, education, and financial services to more than 61 million people annually.

$241.38—For each year over ten years, they could **end malnutrition on planet Earth (World Bank Group, 2016).**

Giving is good for business, but that's not why we do it. We give because it's *who we are.* "The best philanthropy," John D. Rockefeller once wrote, "is constantly in search of finalities—a search for a cause, an attempt to cure evils at their source." This message speaks to us. Our entrepreneurial spirit ensures that the more we give, the better we'll get, until we ultimately overcome the challenges that confront us. This isn't far-fetched. While it has long been thought that the problems charities confront are insurmountable, we must start viewing them as *solvable* because as simple math indicates, they are. The type of giving required is merely an extension of the way small businesses already go above and beyond to provide for our employees and customers. We can use our generosity to define who we are, and as our small businesses become big businesses, we can change the very idea of what it means to be a large company in America.

The time has come for America's entrepreneurs to take their place on the world stage. We don't have to be wealthy or especially accomplished to do so, but we may very well become both of those things as a result. We cannot wait until we're finished to consider our legacy. For our sake and the sake of those in need around the world, we must build it and live it now.

—Christopher Andrus
December 19, 2017, to October 4, 2019

LET'S ACTUALLY CHANGE THE WORLD

....

"ANY MINUTE, ANY DAY, SOME PLAYERS MAY
BREAK A LONG STANDING RECORD. THAT'S ONE
OF THE FASCINATIONS ABOUT THE GAME,
THE UNEXPECTED SURPRISES."
— CONNIE MACK

THIRTY-THREE DOLLARS AND thirty-three cents. That's how much it will cost each of America's small businesses to permanently change one of our nation's great nonprofits. It's just as easy as it sounds.

In 2018, I was honored to be named the West Michigan Leukemia and Lymphoma Society's "Man of the Year" by raising nearly $33,000 for the cause. During the ten-week fundraising period, I spent a lot of time meeting survivors of blood cancers. My only connection with the cause prior to that point had been my cousin Ellie—who was diagnosed with acute lymphoblastic leukemia when she was in high school—but I quickly learned how much the disease had touched nearly everyone around me in some way. It was an eye-opening experience, and it bonded me to their mission forever.

LLS is a vital and irreplaceable organization. Though it's a nationwide nonprofit, it touches nearly every local community. I spent some time studying its history and learned that as a direct result of its efforts, survival rates for certain types of blood cancer have quadrupled, and nearly all of today's most promising cancer treatments were advanced by its research. Since its founding in 1949, the LLS has made a cumulative research investment of $1.2 billion and changed the expectation of what it means to be diagnosed with blood cancer.

At a certain point in the campaign—during which I was also working on this book—I calculated that a one-time $33.33 donation from each of America's 30 million small businesses could match nearly seventy years of LLS's research fundraising *in one day*.

Think about that.

The amount of $33.33 is all but a rounding error, even for small companies. For us, that's six pints of beer—or two pizzas. I imagined it through the lens of our small business neighbors. It was eight ice cream cones from Furniture City Creamery. One pair of sandals from Mieras Family Shoes. Two #3 combo meals from Two Scotts Barbecue. One T-shirt from the Mitten State. Five specialty juices at Malamiah Juice Bar. And so on, and so on.

I've spent the preceding pages making a case for entrepreneur-driven small businesses being America's most trusted entities, and I've illustrated their combined giving potential. We now stand at the precipice of a great opportunity to realize that potential. The intersection of America's most numerous business type and the largest buying generation ever to walk the earth provides an opportunity to aim America's wealth in an extraordinary direction.

We are calling on the small businesses of America to join together to help our nonprofits *actually accomplish their goals.* Whether it's curing blood cancer, providing services for wounded veterans, granting wishes for sick children, or one of the myriad other challenges America's nonprofits confront daily, the chances of achieving this have never been more real. As we learn from "The Parable of the River," the last phase of meaningful work is *a change in perspective,* not effort. This insignificant $33.33 sum proves that giving on a meaningful level doesn't require any amount of accumulation. These 30 million individual gifts joined together can become as much as $1 billion, and each year that goes by can see a different cause infused with enough cash to actually move the needle on its mission, not merely chip away at it. The price tag ensures this effort doesn't have to come at the cost of ignoring *any* other responsibilities.

The world doesn't need more nonprofits. It needs to better serve the ones it already has. And small businesses can do exactly that. Cause by cause, we can secure our place in America's history by allowing nonprofits to fulfill their missions. We can liberate them from their burdensome fundraising challenges and bring their important work to its tipping point.

To learn more, visit *christopherandrus.com* and read about "The 3333 Promise."

OUR PARTNERS SPEAK

....

"My experience in community work and nonprofit leadership has centered on resident engagement, family support, and collaboration. The grassroots nature and service-based core of nonprofit efforts are as messy as they are beautiful. The relationships and meaningful moments that flood the work itself keep underpaid and overworked employees committed and enthusiastic. These wonderful realities can easily get lost in the midst of funding campaigns, grant writing, and corporate reporting. The names and faces of those people impacted by nonprofit services go missing in the lists of data and charts. Mitten Foundation is an astonishingly different support mechanism altogether.

Chris Andrus and Max Trierweiler have struck gold in their local business at Leonard and Quarry St. I do not mean to imply that the Mitten Brewing Co.'s amazing beers and out-of-this-world pizzas are simply a financial windfall, although I truly hope that to be the case. I am speaking directly to the effort they have made as owners in their hiring practices, their community engagement, their neighborly demeanor, their inclusive business model, their local support, and their willingness to dream bigger.

Mitten Foundation stems directly from the ownership and the management's heart for community. Dana, Mallory, Chris, Max, and many more alongside them have been paving the way in what seems so simple but feels revolutionary. This company has sacrificed time, staff, money, and energy to redirect efforts from their growing business to additionally help their local community grow alongside them. Reimagining the ways a local restaurant/brewery could support its neighbors, their foundation and its board of directors look to local service agencies to support grassroots, street-level initiatives that are making difference or significantly working to sustain impact in the neighborhoods the Mitten is proud to be a part of.

I cannot find the words to say how courageous I think this commitment has been. The nonprofit community rejoices in these efforts. The local residents celebrate this foundation, dedicating even more loyalty and appreciation for the team at Mitten Brewing as they learn more and more about how the business is supporting the challenging and tireless work happening day in and day out among neighbors.

Mitten Foundation brings financial support, community advocacy, and project resources to the table, while shifting the philanthropy model from lists, charts, outcomes, and indicators, and instead recognizes the faces of the initiatives. Mitten Foundation celebrates the local nature of the nonprofit efforts and embraces the messiness and convoluted measurements struggling to distinguish success from failure. Their ability to meet organizations in authentic conversations about efforts, initiatives, and challenges puts community back in the conversation of fund development.

I would be more than happy to go on and on and on . . . should you have questions, need clarification, or find interest in the beautiful relationship the Mitten Foundation has with its community. I have been affected personally. My nonprofit work has specifically been supported. Moreover, my neighbors, the names, families, and faces of my community, have benefited as a direct result of this beautiful concept.

I believe the model they have championed is one more local leaders should adopt. The mutual benefits seem to be countless, and the energies created by the foundation are palpable in the building itself. You can almost taste it in the pizza. You can hear it in the clinking of the glasses."

Cheers.

—*Jim Davis, Executive Director,*
Westside Collaborative

....

"As a small nonprofit and being new to the community, it took a bit of time [for us] to figure out how to gain the support needed to endure. In the process, I also discovered that not only is the fiscal goal important, but the mission is as well. There are many ways to meet your mission, not all of them being financial.

We found through the early years that being a part of our community was the most important part of our mission, so we made it a point to be a part of the small business and small nonprofit arena. It helps to gather understanding and determine goals to be 'in' a community. Every step of our way has fostered relationships and awareness, which we hope in the end will garner possibilities for the individuals we serve as a nonprofit.

The help of a local business in sponsoring supplies or an event allows us to reach and grow our programs. For businesses to give to a local nonprofit, it means they are, in a respect, thanking the community by supporting it. It also in the long run furthers the reach and impact of their gifts. The nonprofit has the fiscal responsibility to be effective and utilize funds in the best way possible for all of those involved.

Partnering with a small business such as the Mitten Brewing Company furthers the support to both organizations. It allows for the growth and blooming of ideas, pairing of resources, and the ability to do good. Although it may at times seem little, as a director and a person who always has to ask, having a partnership allows me to have a moment to breathe and move on to the mission of the work we do. I struggle with the time I have to spend being creative and asking for funds; when a business steps up and lends a hand, that secures ideas into plans and hopes into real possibilities. Our nonprofit relies on community, and we want to be a part of it. There are days that a gift from a partner is enough to keep us going. The long-term effect is always multiplied in the community with partnerships."

—*Delight Lester, Executive Director,*
Arts in Motion

Side note: As a one person staff, I do not have the resources of the "big" named nonprofits in town, so I am thrilled by the gifts of all of the businesses that have honored our students by caring and sharing support!

....

"When I think of the Mitten, I think of community engagement and a selfless sense of duty. By this, I simply mean that the Mitten has made a focus of not only being a part of the community, but utilizing its base to do good for those within that community. Over the years, big names have always made their way as the forefront of philanthropy. There are guidelines, but always that sense of the bottom line. With the Mitten, it feels organic and not a sense of 'I have to,' but rather a desire to make sure that while the business thrives, so does the local community.

I have always been blown away by the businesses of the West Side, the Mitten included. When it comes to taking care of those close, there doesn't seem to be a second thought on making sure they have necessities so that they can focus on other things in their lives. Take food and home heating credits—the cost of these can keep people up at night, wondering how they are going to feed their families or stay warm, while the bills still pile on. Providing relief allows people to focus their attention on other things—jobs, children, enjoying life. The Mitten has worked to allow people that sense of not always being focused on the bottom line and just getting by.

In my time working with you all, I have never been so in awe of the eagerness to make others' lives better—and you all do it with a smile. It is what sets some businesses apart from others—that sense of care that I believe everyone should have for their fellow neighbors. The Mitten is not selfish. It does not discriminate. It sees a need and assesses its ability to get involved."

—*Sean Little, Development Manager,*
Feeding America West Michigan

....

"Dear Friends at Mitten Foundation,

I am Carol Manos, director and founder of Carol's Ferals. We are a 501(c)(3) nonprofit operating out of Grand Rapids, serving the West Michigan community with Trap Neuter Return services.

It is our mission to end feline overpopulation through community education and empowerment.

We have been very fortunate to have the Mitten hold two very lucrative fundraisers for our work in saving the lives of cats.

Doing good work is HARD. Finding the money to do the work is getting even HARDER!

When Mitten Foundation chooses to benefit an organization, it gives the organization a big boost, not only in much-needed financial income, but by creating visibility in the area.

We can talk a blue streak about TNR and how we help community cats, but it really lends a great deal of credence to our work when others say it. It says, 'We feel this is a worthy cause.' When our work is seen as good and necessary by a thriving business in Grand Rapids, more people take it seriously. It's not just another crazy cat lady talking, it's a real shot in the arm, and it gives the impression of worthiness. And that is HUGE! And no money can buy THAT!

Our funding from the two events hosted by the Mitten has amounted to more than $6,000. When you look at the impact that just $40 can make by sterilizing one cat on the streets and circumventing the unwanted, unnecessary birth of 11,000 kittens over the course of just five years, you can see that multiplying that amount, exponentially, has a very big pay-off.

Carol's Ferals is very proud to be chosen as a beneficiary of Mitten Foundation. We also really dig the fact that they have vegan options. So not only do they benefit cats with their events for us, they make a difference daily by offering delicious alternatives to meat and dairy.

We absolutely love our Mitten!

—*Carol Manos, Director and Founder,*
Carol's Ferals

. . . .

"If you were to put all eleven of our wheelchair-using young adult residents from Olivia's Gift (OG) in the Mitten Brewery, there might not be enough room for anyone else to walk or sit! They all travel with caregivers and various feeding apparatus, backpacks, and other assistive equipment.

It would be easy for business, especially small business, to ignore these folks. Or hope they won't visit in those numbers, with that equipment. They are not, after all, your usual potential customers.

But the Mitten Foundation took a different approach. Your attention and caring made a difference in two huge ways: It's provided an opportunity for us parents and families to gather on behalf of our kids and enjoy a new way of helping us all with necessary funding; and, second, the dollars have assisted us in providing options for our kids to engage in their community and have the community participate within OG. These funds are being used as part of an effort to repurpose an attached garage into a studio/workshop to be utilized for creative projects that involve making hand-made items for sale in the community!

Watch us grow and participate in the GR community . . . and thanks, Mitten Foundation, for your great help!"

—*Chuck Saur*
Olivia's Gift

. . . .

"The Whitecaps Community Foundation values its relationships with partners in West Michigan that have the same goals of enriching the lives of children and their families in our area. The

Mitten Brewing Company fits the bill of a good partner in every sense of the word. Not only do we love our partners that help us celebrate what the value of a dollar can do to help our community, but we love the Mitten Brewing Company's passion for the sport of baseball. What is most special about our partnership with the Mitten Brewing Company is that it happened so organically without ever a true ask, which speaks to the power of our West Michigan community. Max and Chris heard about our program and found a way to help us make a difference. The proceeds from the Ted Rasberry fund have helped us make sure that we can continue to provide a completely free opportunity to fall in love with the sport we all love, baseball."

—*Jessica Muzevuca, Community Relations Manager,*
Whitecaps Community Foundation

. . . .

"Since its inception, Mitten Foundation has meant the world to Comprehensive Therapy Center. It has allowed us to be visible in the community, provided an opportunity for our families who would not otherwise be able to afford fund raising, and helped us raise much-needed resources for families who have children with disabilities. The need for resources continues to increase amid decreases in philanthropy. The Mitten Brewing Company fancies itself as a small business, but to Comprehensive Therapy Center, it is a huge benefactor in our continued success."

—*Jean Silbar, Executive Director,*
Comprehensive Therapy Center

. . . .

"Partnering with the Mitten Foundation has greatly benefitted Autism Support of Kent County. As a small nonprofit that depends entirely on donations, we are grateful to receive financial support from the Mitten. The amount that it gives us, through the Autism Support Night at the Mitten, is meaningful to our programs and services. In addition, partnering with the Mitten has given us exposure to its customers. Being able to align ourselves with a growing organization just helps us look better. Finally, the Mitten has always treated our autism families extremely well. To invite our families, who may not be able to get out much, to a special night is important. Because they feel comfortable eating at and enjoying time at the Mitten on our special Autism Support Night, they are more likely to return to the restaurant. Being able to feel comfortable bringing a family member with autism there is truly a gift that the staff at the Mitten has given to our families.

Thank you, Mitten Foundation, for your presence in Grand Rapids!"

—*Pam Liggett, Executive Director,*
Autism Support of Kent County

....

"Working with the Mitten Foundation has been a bright spot in my work so far. It has been truly amazing to work with Chris and Dana. I am consistently amazed by the generosity and willingness to support our families and students here. It's also been good for me personally, as I have had to check myself and how I view businesses. It's hard for me to put into words really, but my work with the Mitten Foundation has been a continued source of inspiration for me. I feel more confident, and I feel I have an ace up my sleeve [because] when I really need something, I can reach out, and we can brainstorm solutions and get results. I love that you come and hand out pizza to the families during the Mobile Food Trucks. It's little things like that, when I look back and reflect, that I feel have a real impact on our community that we are serving, and now we are serving that community together. I appreciate all that you and the Mitten Foundation have done, and I get excited when I think about the future. I have a small dream to someday work under Dana and help support the vision of the Mitten Foundation. :-)

Cheers to you and all that you do. Our world needs more people and businesses like yours."

—*Stephen Lovell, Community School Coordinator,*
Kent School Services Network—A Community School Coalition

WORKS CITED

....

Author's Note

Howton, Elizabeth. 2018. "Nearly Half the World Lives on Less Than $5.50 a Day." The World Bank. October 17, 2018. https://www.worldbank.org/en/news/press-release/2018/10/17/nearly-half-the-world-lives-on-less-than-550-a-day.

Introduction

FAS Arizona. 2018. "The Story of the River Babies." http://fasarizona.com/riverbabies.htm, accessed on January 15, 2018.

Charity Navigator. 2018. "Giving Statistics." https://www.charitynavigator.org/index.cfm?bay=content.view&cpid=42.

Osili, Una, and Sasha Zarins. 2018. "Fewer Americans Are Giving Money to Charity but Total Donations Are at Record Levels Anyway." *The Conversation*. July 3, 2018. http://theconversation.com/fewer-americans-are-giving-money-to-charity-but-total-donations-are-at-record-levels-anyway-98291.

Stern, Ken. 2013. "Why the Rich Don't Give to Charity." *The Atlantic*. April 2013. https://www.theatlantic.com/magazine/archive/2013/04/why-the-rich-dont-give/309254/.

Swanson, Ana. 2016. "America's Biggest Charity Is No Longer What Most People Think of as a Charity." *Washington Post.* October 27, 2016. https://www.washingtonpost.com/news/wonk/wp/2016/10/27/americas-biggest-charity-is-no-longer-what-most-people-think-of-as-a-charity/.

Te, Nhu. 2017. "Rise of the Donor-Advised Fund: A Fast-Growing Vehicle to Charitable Giving." *NonProfit PRO.* May 25, 2017. https://www.nonprofitpro.com/article/rise-donor-advised-fund/.

Miller, Lisa. 2012. "The Money-Empathy Gap." *New York Magazine.* June 29, 2012. http://nymag.com/news/features/money-brain-2012-7/.

SBA Office of Advocacy. 2018. "2018 Small Business Profile." U.S. Small Business Administration. https://www.sba.gov/sites/default/files/advocacy/2018-Small-Business-Profiles-US.pdf.

Sophy, Joshua. 2016. "42 Percent of Small Businesses Give Up to $1,000 to Charity and Prefer to Give Cash." *Small Business Trends.* https://smallbiztrends.com/2016/12/small-business-donations.html.

Cone Communications. 2017. "2017 Cone Communications CSR Study." http://www.conecomm.com/research-blog/2017-csr-study.

Fry, Richard. 2018. "Millennials Projected to Overtake Baby Boomers as America's Largest Generation." Pew Research Center. March 1, 2018. https://www.pewresearch.org/fact-tank/2018/03/01/millennials-overtake-baby-boomers/.

Chapter 1

Levy, Darlene Ann. 2012. "Helping Those in Need around the Holidays." Purdue University. December 3, 2012. https://www.purdueglobal.edu/blog/social-behavioral-sciences/helping-those-in-need/.

Sugirtharajah, Sharada. 2001. "Traditions of Giving in Hinduism." *Alliance Magazine.* September 1, 2001. https://www.alliancemagazine.org/feature/traditions-of-giving-in-hinduism/.

Winchester, Donald. 2015. "Thomas Aquinas: In the Light of Human Reason." *Vision*. Fall 2015. https://www.vision.org/thomas-aquinas-biography-human-reasoning-2973.

Kant, Immanuel. 1785. *The Groundwork for the Metaphysics of Morals*.

Brooks, Rebecca Beatrice. 2012. "Squanto: The Former Slave." *History of Massachusetts*. September 28, 2012. https://historyofmassachusetts.org/squanto-the-former-slave/.

De Tocqueville, Alexis. 1835. *Democracy in America.*

Chapter 3
Perry, Suzanne. 2013. "The Stubborn 2% Giving Rate." *Chronicle of Philanthropy*. June 17, 2013. https://www.philanthropy.com/article/The-Stubborn-2-Giving-Rate/154691.

Fromm, Jeff. 2018. "Understanding the New Rules of Philanthropy in a Millennial Age." *Forbes*. February 27, 2018. https://www.forbes.com/sites/jefffromm/2018/02/27/understanding-the-new-rules-of-philanthropy-in-a-millennial-age/.

Chapter 4
Feeding America. 2018. "Senior Hunger Poses Unique Challenges." https://www.feedingamerica.org/hunger-in-america/senior-hunger-facts, accessed on March 15, 2018.

Chapter 5
Effective Altruism. 2016. "Introduction to Effective Altruism." June 22, 2016. https://www.effectivealtruism.org/articles/introduction-to-effective-altruism/.

Chapter 6

Lencioni, Patrick M. 2002. "Make Your Values Mean Something." *Harvard Business Review*. July 2002. https://hbr.org/2002/07/make-your-values-mean-something.

Gordon, John Steele. 2017. "John Rockefeller Sr." Philanthropy Roundtable. https://www.philanthropyroundtable.org/almanac/people/hall-of-fame/detail/john-rockefeller-sr, accessed on December 15, 2017.

Chapter 7

Restaurant Den. 2019. "Advice from Jon Taffer on Why Customer Service Matters." https://restaurantden.com/why-customer-service-matters/, accessed on July 16, 2019.

Chapter 8

Salmon, Jacqueline L. 2008. "Church Mission Trips May Hurt the Ones They're Trying to Help." *Daily News*. July 19, 2008. https://tdn.com/lifestyles/church-mission-trips-may-hurt-the-ones-they-re-trying/article_d10e9c52-d3d6-5e58-9eec-3940df0c1c93.html.

ATD Fourth World USA. 2018. "Poverty Myth: Poor People Don't Want to Work. FALSE!" April 5, 2018. https://4thworldmovement.org/poverty-myths-busted-poor-people-dont-want-work/.

Wadhams, Nick. 2010. "Bad Charity? (All I Got Was This Lousy T-Shirt!)" *Time*. May 12, 2010. http://content.time.com/time/world/article/0,8599,1987628,00.html.

Natural Resources Defense Council. 2018. "Food Waste." https://www.nrdc.org/issues/food-waste, accessed on January 25, 2018.

Yglesias, Matthew. 2011. "Can the Cans." *Slate*. December 7, 2011. https://slate.com/business/2011/12/food-drives-charities-need-your-money-not-your-random-old-food.html.

Conan, Neil. 2011. "A Case for Cash Donations, instead of Cans." NPR. November 22, 2011. https://www.npr.org/2011/11/22/142661882/a-case-for-cash-donations-instead-of-cans.

Kids' Food Basket. 2018. "Supper Packs." https://www.kidsfoodbasket.org/opportunities/supper-packs/, accessed on December 11, 2018.

May, Kate Torgovnick. 2014. "Correcting the Overhead Myth: How Dan Pallotta's TED Talk Has Begun to Change the Conversation." TED Blog. March 13, 2014. https://blog.ted.com/correcting-the-overhead-myth-how-dan-pallottas-ted-talk-has-begun-to-change-the-conversation/.

Lynch, Loreal. 2010. "Suing for the Cure?" *Stanford Social Innovation Review*. August 11, 2010. https://ssir.org/articles/entry/suing_for_the_cure.

Chapter 9

Huang, Wayne, John Mitchell, Carmel Dibner, Andrea Ruttenberg, and Audrey Tripp. 2018. "How Customer Service Can Turn Angry Customers into Loyal Ones." *Harvard Business Review*. January 16, 2018. https://hbr.org/2018/01/how-customer-service-can-turn-angry-customers-into-loyal-ones.

Rock, David. 2009. "Managing with the Brain in Mind." *strategy+business*. August 27, 2009. https://www.strategy-business.com/article/09306?gko=9efb2.

Tabibnia, Golnaz, Ajay B. Satpute, and Matthew D. Lieberman. 2008. "The Sunny Side of Fairness." Association for Psychological Science. http://www.wcas.northwestern.edu/nescan/TabibniaSatputeLieberman2008.pdf.

Ramey, Corinne, and Bob Tita. 2018. "The Summer of Plastic-Straw Bans: How We Got There." *Wall Street Journal*. August 7, 2018. https://www.wsj.com/articles/the-summer-of-plastic-straw-bans-how-we-got-there-1533634200.

Vallely, Erin. 2019. "Grasping at Straws: The Ableism of the Straw Ban." Center for Disability Rights. http://cdrnys.org/blog/disability-dialogue/ grasping-at-straws-the-ableism-of-the-straw-ban/, accessed on July 16, 2019.

Ford Motor Company. 2018. "Looking Further with Ford." https:// media.ford.com/content/dam/fordmedia/North%20America/ US/2016/.12/7/2017-Looking%20-Further-with-Ford-Trend-Report.pdf.

Jeltsen, Melissa. "Chick-Fil-A Has 'Record-Setting Day' While Embroiled in Anti-Gay Controversy." 2012. *Huffington Post.* August 2, 2012. https://www.huffpost.com/entry/chick-fil-a-has-record-setting-day-anti-gay_n_1733697.

Graham, Ruth. 2019. "The Uncanceling of Chick-Fil-A." *Slate.* March 7, 2019. https://slate.com/human-interest/2019/03/chick-fil-a-boycott-liberals-forgot-chicken-too-good.html.

Carlock, Catherine. 2010. "Gas-Station Owners, Not BP, Feel Sting of Boycotts." MarketWatch. June 22, 2010. https://www.marketwatch.com/story/bp-boycott-hits-gas-station-owners-hardest-2010-06-22.

Weber Shandwick, Inc. 2018. "Battle of the Wallets: The Changing Landscape of Consumer Activism." January 30, 2018. https://www.webershandwick.com/news/battle-of-the-wallets-the-changing-landscape-of-consumer-activism/.

Chapter 10

LIHEAP. 2018. "President's Budget Request Eliminates LIHEAP Funding despite Congressional Support." February 12, 2018. https://www.liheap.org/news/2018/2/12/presidents-budget-request-eliminates-liheap-funding-despite-congressional-support.

Chapter 11

Lofton, Justine. 2019. "Another Michigan Brewery Pays Off School Lunch Debts for Students." *MLive.* August 23, 2019. https://www.mlive.com/news/muskegon/2019/08/another-michigan-brewery-pays-off-school-lunch-debts-for-students.html.

Grabowski, Ken. 2019. "Big Hearts: LRCR School Lunch Debt Fund Drive Surpasses Goal." *Manistee News Advocate.* October 1, 2019. https://www.manisteenews.com/local-news/article/Big-hearts-14484282.php.

Snider, Mike. 2018. "More Than 1,200 Breweries Answer Sierra Nevada's Call for Camp Fire Relief Beer." *USA Today.* November 28, 2018. https://www.usatoday.com/story/money/business/2018/11/28/camp-fire-relief-beer-brewed-sierra-nevada-and-1-000-others/2124195002/.

van der Linden, Sander. 2017. "The Surprisingly Short Life of Viral Social Movements." *Scientific American.* February 15, 2017. https://www.scientificamerican.com/article/the-surprisingly-short-life-of-viral-social-movements/.

Wells Fargo Works. 2018. "Wells Fargo Survey: Small Business Optimism Soars on Strong Revenues and Cash Flow." December 4, 2018. https://wellsfargoworks.com/insights/press-release/small-business-optimism-soars-on-strong-revenues-and-cash-flow.

Chapter 12

Elkington, John. 2018. "25 Years Ago I Coined the Phrase 'Triple Bottom Line.' Here's Why It's Time to Rethink It." *Harvard Business Review.* June 25, 2018. https://hbr.org/2018/06/25-years-ago-i-coined-the-phrase-triple-bottom-line-heres-why-im-giving-up-on-it.

Bishop, Bill. "Americans Have Lost Faith in Institutions. That's Not because of Trump or Fake News." 2017. *Washington Post.* March 3, 2017. https://www.washingtonpost.com/posteverything/wp/2017/03/03/americans-have-lost-faith-in-institutions-thats-not-because-of-trump-or-fake-news/.

Prahalad, C. K. 2017. "Why America Has a Trust Problem." *The Economist.* August 25, 2017. https://www.economist.com/democracy-in-america/2017/04/25/why-america-has-a-trust-problem.

U.S. Small Business Administration. 2018. "What's New with Small Business?" August 2018. https://www.sba.gov/sites/default/files/Whats-New-With-Small-Business-2018.pdf.

Forbes. 2018. "The 100 Largest U.S. Charities." https://www.forbes.com/top-charities/list/.

World Bank Group. 2016. "Reaching the Global Target to Reduce Stunting: How Much Will It Cost and How Can We Pay for It?" http://documents.worldbank.org/curated/en/963161467989517289/pdf/104865-REVISED-Investing-in-Nutrition-FINAL.pdf.